My Intense Emotions Handbook

My Intense Emotions Handbook

Manage Your Emotions and Connect Better with Others

Sue Knowles, Bridie Gallagher
and Hannah Bromley

Foreword by Kim S. Golding

Illustrated by Emmeline Pidgen

Jessica Kingsley Publishers
London and Philadelphia

First published in Great Britain in 2021 by Jessica Kingsley Publishers
An Hachette Company

3

Copyright © Sue Knowles, Bridie Gallagher and Hannah Bromley 2021

A CIP catalogue record for this title is available from the
British Library and the Library of Congress

ISBN 978 1 78775 382 2
eISBN 978 1 78775 383 9

Printed and bound in Great Britain by Clays Ltd, Elcograf S.p.A.

Jessica Kingsley Publishers' policy is to use papers that are natural,
renewable and recyclable products and made from wood grown in
sustainable forests. The logging and manufacturing processes are expected
to conform to the environmental regulations of the country of origin.

Jessica Kingsley Publishers
Carmelite House
50 Victoria Embankment
London EC4Y 0DZ

www.jkp.com

Contents

FOREWORD

Kim S. Golding

He would come to her at the most inconvenient of times, whispering in her ear, telling her to be careful of this, to look out for that, to worry about the other. He got into her head and then she would be flooded with anxiety, fear and worries. This made her feel very sad. She didn't want these feelings anymore. She called him 'Bottle, Bottle, Bang' because this is what he did. He encouraged her to bottle up all of her feelings; keep a tight lid on them and then 'bang' they would flood out of her. Sometimes she wanted him to leave her alone, but she was afraid. If he wasn't around, how would she cope? For good or bad 'Bottle, Bottle Bang' was a part of her.

I wonder if you have a 'Bottle, Bottle, Bang' who whispers in your ear. Perhaps you have a different name for him. Maybe you haven't thought of it in this way. Do you experience a pressure to manage lots of feelings by trying to make them go away, dreading the moment you can't do this anymore and they burst from you, startling people around you? Or maybe, for you, these pesky feelings are always there running your life. Many people struggle to understand and cope with lots of strong feelings, and sometimes it can feel as if the feelings control them. If you recognize any of this, then I think this book is for you.

Emotions are an important part of us; they add colour to what would otherwise be a black and white world. They make exciting things enjoyable; they warn us when we might be in danger; they let us know when we are having a hard time and need to take care of ourselves. We are all born experiencing these emotions but we must learn how to handle them. Just like learning to handle words when we learn to read and write or numbers when we learn maths, we have to learn to recognize and control the feelings that are always with us. Right from when we are born, our parents, or those caring closely for us, are helping us to understand what we are feeling and are helping us to regulate these feelings. They soothe our negative emotions and share and enjoy our positive ones. As we grow up, we learn to put words to these experiences, and we get better at regulating them for ourselves. For some of us, this is more difficult. We might have parents who are not very good at helping their children with this; perhaps because they didn't get good help when they were little. We might have been born with some super strong emotional responses that are hard to manage without a lot of extra support. We might have had a lot more stress than we can cope with because of things that have happened to us. There are lots of reasons why our feelings can be tricky to live with. We all need extra support sometimes, and some of us need to look hard to find out what works for us.

Sue, Bridie and Hannah have written a book that is full of ideas for understanding and managing when our emotions are difficult to cope with. Not all of these will be helpful. You need to find out what works for you. In this book, you will get loads of ideas that you can try out to see what fits. You will find ideas about what emotions are and why we need them. You will learn to recognize how you manage them when they become tricky, and how this can cause even more problems for you. There are lots of ways to help us live with our emotions, to soothe them, to ride the storm when they will not be soothed and to generally take care of ourselves so that our feelings become easier on us. Sometimes, our emotions can cause problems for us with other people. This book also gives ideas for this, including how we recognize what others are feeling, learn to let them know we get it, and how we can be assertive about what we need. Looking after relationships that are important to us, repairing these relationships when we meet sticky patches and getting out of relationships that are not good for us all involve understanding and managing emotions.

You have picked this book up, so you are already working hard to figure out this emotional stuff. Sometimes this means letting other people help us as well as finding ways to take better care of ourselves. I think that as you do this you will learn a lot about your feelings and how to be kind and caring to yourself. Emotions are there to help us in all sorts of ways, but they can get a bit carried away sometimes. In this book, I hope you find help to work with your emotions so that you can get the best from them, learning to be compassionate and caring for yourself along the way.

'Bottle, Bottle Bang' wanted to help her. He knew he had an important job to do to help her to survive. He wanted to carry out this job as best he could. Sometimes she was angry with him and this made him sad and worried. 'Bottle, Bottle, Bang' wasn't sure what to do. He tried even harder to point out all the things that might cause her trouble, until she was so full of anxiety, fear and worries she didn't know what to do with herself. They needed help. She found a book that explained all about emotions, and she began to understand how 'Bottle, Bottle, Bang' was a part of her brain that was trying to help her. She felt grateful for his efforts and glad that he was there looking out for her. She also became better at letting him know when he could step down, and that she was doing OK. They learned to take good care of her, and the emotional storms got easier. She didn't call him 'Bottle, Bottle, Bang' anymore. She was no longer trying to bottle these emotions until she went bang. They had figured out how to work as a team, managing feelings so that they didn't overwhelm her, and seeking help when this got a bit much. She didn't need to make feelings go away anymore.

Acknowledgements

Our biggest thank you goes to all the young people who have contributed to this book in some way, whether they know it or not. It's through their wisdom and guidance, the sharing of their stories and personal examples, and through their grammatical skills that we made it happen. We couldn't have done with this without you.

Sue would like to thank her husband Ben for his ongoing support, patience and foot rubs; her son Tom for reading through her endless chapter drafts (still for ice-cream); her Aunty P for always believing in her, and her two adorable dogs, who are happy to keep her company (sit on her feet) when she's writing. Bridie has a big thank you for all her family, friends and colleagues for all the co-regulation and riding the waves with her, and an extra huge thank you to Chris, Reuben and Anna for putting up with some intense emotions and bringing so much joy, as well as occasional rage. Hannah would like to say thank you to her mum and dad, who have always been by her side helping her to fight her battles. She'd also like to say thank you to Grace and Alice, who make her feel loved, in her good days and her crazy days.

We are grateful and thankful to Kim Golding for writing the brilliant foreword, for her encouragement, inspiration and support, and for just being her.

Huge thanks and appreciation to Dr Turlough Mills for being the 'real' doctor in the book and generously sharing his wisdom and medication know-how. Thank you to Ben Dawson, our wonderful clinical neuropsychologist, who made sure that we were talking sense in our brain chapter. A big thank you to our draft readers, Steve and Charlene, for their feedback and enthusiasm. Thanks to Sarah Handley for her wisdom on mentalizing (for the book and just generally). We also wanted to acknowledge the amazing contributions from our illustrator Emmeline, who has been with us from the start and has created some beautiful illustrations that have brought our writing to life.

≥ Part 1 ≤

UNDERSTANDING OUR EMOTIONS AND RELATIONSHIPS

In Part 1, we start to explore and understand *why* we might feel such intense emotions. Where might they come from? Why do we perhaps seem to struggle more with emotions than our friends or family? Is there something wrong with us? We think about what 'normal' development looks like, and how the changes that we go through during adolescence (as our brains go through a complete renovation) can influence this. Then we start to think about relationships, how our early life experiences can impact on how we cope with difficult emotions, and how we understand ourselves, our relationships with others and the world around us. So, Part 1 is all about self-exploration and getting to know ourselves a bit better.

≳ Chapter 1 ≲

So, What's This Book All About?

Why write a book about emotions?

We wrote this book because we know, and work with, *many* young people who are struggling to cope with overwhelming emotions that can lead to some risky behaviours. Psychologists, teachers and doctors sometimes call this 'emotional dysregulation' (finding it hard to calm emotions and feel OK again). We know that intense emotions can be associated with lots of different problems like self-harm, angry outbursts, traumatic stress and relationship issues. We also know that if you have neurodevelopmental differences, like difficulties with social communication, impulse control, attention or concentration, then this can make experiencing and managing emotions trickier. There might be more frustration due to living in a world designed for 'neurotypical' people, and the way that emotions and relationships work can just be more uncomfortable or challenging. We hope that having a guide with lots of ideas about how to feel more in control of feelings and relationships will be helpful.

We also wrote this book because we know that for just about everyone at some point in their lives, intense emotions will be hard to handle and a little help is required. We are well aware that many people struggle with their emotions without letting anyone know, and that we're not all lucky enough to have been taught about our emotions and how to handle them when we were growing up. Even for those of us who did learn about this, life can throw tough things our way that overwhelm the coping and regulation strategies that we have. As we get older, relationships get a lot more complicated so we need to understand our emotions to stay healthy and develop our ways to feel OK.

We learn about emotions before we can even talk and often without being consciously aware of it. So, it can feel weird thinking and talking about emotions, especially if this isn't something you are used to doing in your family. This is one of the other reasons we wanted to write a friendly guide book, with some real-life stories of hope and resilience, which can be alongside you as you explore (at your own pace) where your intense emotions come from and how they affect you and your relationships. We wanted to provide some ideas about ways to manage these in a healthy, positive way. We don't imagine you'll sit down and read this book in one go, or even three goes. It is written so you can dip in and out of the chapters as you need to and pick up the strategies and ideas that fit with where you're at.

Is this book able to help with self-harm and other 'risky behaviours'?

When people struggle with intense emotions, they haven't found ways to soothe themselves when they get overwhelmed or life gets stressful. If you can't self-soothe, you have to find other ways to try to cope with intense emotions and this can be through injuring yourself, using substances (like drugs or alcohol), being very controlling of your environment and relationships to feel safe, or seeking out very risky environments and relationships to feel...something. We don't talk specifically about self-harm and substance use in the book, because there are resources available, *but* all of the ideas and techniques in the book are ones that we use when working with young people who are struggling with harming themselves or using substances, often in an attempt to cope with intense emotions.

Can you help me only feel the good emotions?

If you've picked up this book, then emotions are probably causing you some problems. But it's important to remember that *all* emotions are a vital part of being human. Emotions give us essential information that lets us know that something is happening and we need to pay attention. Emotions can be used to communicate important information to other people without us even realizing (through our body language or facial expression), and can influence how they react to us. They can also let *us* know if we need to react to something and can get us ready to act. Importantly, if we were under some sort of threat, we would suddenly feel fear and this would activate our survival response, getting us ready to fight, flight (run away) or freeze (on the spot). This keeps us safe when there is a physical threat like a predator, but also lets us know when something isn't right in our lives. So remember, the emotions that can feel worst keep you alive! Emotions can also motivate you to act in particularly helpful ways. The feeling of guilt may make you want to repair a relationship or situation, or the feeling of disgust might get you far away from some horrible thing that will make you sick. Maybe, most importantly, they can be fun and keep life interesting. Imagine a life without emotions...we would all act more like robots.

So, some emotions feel amazing, like excitement and joy, but then others can feel unbearably painful, like loss and sadness. What we tend to do is lump the emotions that make us feel nice in the 'good section' and those that feel really painful in the 'bad section', which is logical, but emotions are neither good nor bad, they just *are*. The problem is that labelling some 'bad' makes it more likely that we will try to ignore or suppress them – and this never works.

What age range is this book for?

We wrote this book for people who are about 14 or older. We've tried to keep the language as simple as possible, but we try not to be patronizing. We want you to understand some of the complexity behind intense emotions, so it does get a bit complicated. We will use the words 'feelings' and 'emotions' interchangeably, mostly just to stop us sounding too boring and repetitive. We also talk about 'feelings in our bodies' and 'feeling OK in your body' because we're also talking about *sensations* rather than just emotions. This book might best be used with the help of a trusted adult if you're one of our younger readers, but actually, for anyone, it can really help to be able to talk through ideas, get another perspective and seek support. We know that sharing intense emotions and seeking support isn't always easy and we address this through the book too.

How do I know these ideas are worth trying?

To try to help you to understand and manage emotions and relationships, we've used lots of different ideas and theories developed by mental health professionals over the years. We draw on attachment theory, we use dialectical behaviour therapy (DBT) ideas and strategies, some mentalizing, and some cognitive behavioral therapy (CBT) techniques. We also use some compassion-focused therapy (CFT) ideas to help us think about telling your story. We then draw on what we know from theories and research from the field of neurodevelopment so we can think about your brain in adolescence (which we think of as up to the age of 25). We wanted to provide you with a menu of ideas, strategies and techniques that the evidence tells us work for young people (research), that young people tell us work (our expert by experience author Hannah, and all our contributors through their personal stories) and what Sue and Bridie have found to be most useful when young people are struggling to understand and manage emotions and relationships. It means there is a lot to take in, but it also means you've lots to choose from.

Can you guarantee me these ideas will work?

We expect that not all the ideas and strategies help everyone, so some things won't work for you. But it's important to remember that some things might not work first time and need practice, and others need to be left behind (for now, not forever) because they may well be helpful in the future. We talk about patterns of relating and coping, and how falling back into old ways when you are making change is absolutely to be expected. When this happens, you need to be kind to yourself and gently get back on track, because giving yourself a hard time is never helpful. Trying something new is hard, and slip-ups can be seen as chances to learn.

Are you psychologists telling me how I should feel and how to have a 'good' relationship?

One of the things we were keenly aware of when writing this book is how different cultures think about and share emotions (or don't share them). We, the authors, were brought up and are all living in the UK, where, historically, there has been a tradition of not sharing feelings and where stoicism and being self-sufficient are valued in our individualist society. Things are changing a little but it remains an important part of British cultural norms. In other parts of Europe, being very expressive about emotions and very direct is more 'normal', and being passionate and emotional in relationships is valued. In some Asian cultures, there's a real focus on ensuring the comfort of other people and not paying attention to or sharing your own feelings, often meaning that relationships are extremely important but are rule-driven rather than emotion-driven. How and where we grew up, and the rules and expectations of that culture, will have a huge impact on how we understand and manage our feelings, what we hope to be able to achieve when we talk about 'feeling OK in our bodies' and having 'healthy, balanced relationships'. As authors, we can't take ourselves out of our cultural context, but we can be aware of it. This is another reason why we have lots of ideas in the book and why having a trusted adult can be really helpful so that you can have conversations about expectations and behaviours in your own community.

What's actually in the book?

We have split the book into four parts.

In Part 1 (which you've already started reading), we start to explore and understand *why* we might feel such intense emotions. Where might they come from? Why do we perhaps seem to struggle more with emotions than our friends or family? Is there something wrong with us? We'll think about what 'normal' development looks like, and how the changes that we go through during adolescence (as our brains go through a complete renovation) can influence this. Then we'll start to think about relationships, and how our early life experiences can impact on how we cope with difficult emotions, how we understand ourselves, our relationships with others, and the world around us. So, Part 1 is all about self-exploration and getting to know ourselves a bit better.

Breaking it down, Part 1 starts with this introduction and outline of the book and what it's about, then goes on to Chapter 2, What's Wrong With Me?, which discusses the ideas around why some people struggle with intense emotions, why some people seek a diagnosis, the term 'personality disorder' and our ideas about how best to try to understand your difficulties (Formulation and My story). This chapter shares personal experience from a young person about the benefits of this approach and guides you through starting to tell your own story and beginning to understand your own intense emotions, where they might come from, and what could be keeping them going. Chapter 3 gives you a whistle-stop tour of what's going on in your brain during adolescence (remember, 10–25 years) and how this affects your emotions and relationships. Chapters 4 and 5 think about how our early experiences shape the ways we understand and manage our emotions, and how we manage and understand our relationships. Chapter 4, Big Emotions and Relationships, looks at a more anxious and preoccupied style that develops, where we feel as if we need others to be OK, and how we might try to step aside and find new and more balanced ways to cope and relate to others. Chapter 5, Bottle, Bottle, Bang!, looks at what can happen when we bottle up our emotions and how we can start to reconnect with ourselves and others.

In Part 2, we explore coping strategies that can help you to deal with intense emotions. Chapter 6 focuses on getting the basics right, such as sleep, diet and exercise, as we know that these can help us to feel OK in our bodies. We'll then start to think about ways to soothe difficult or painful feelings, coping strategies which will help you to transform or feel more in control of your emotions, and how to cope in a crisis. When reading through Part 2, it might be useful to keep a note of strategies that you find helpful, then you can put them together in a self-care plan at the end of the book. We start with Chapter 6, Getting the Basics Right: Feeling OK in Your Body, so that you're not starting off with the complex stuff without having the foundations in place. We know that when young people come to us in crisis, they think we're idiots going on about sleep, food, breathing, routine and all this other stuff, but it's so important to try to get these things right so that we have a better chance at the other stuff working. We move on to Chapter 7 about self-soothing and finding new ways to soothe and regulate your emotions when they become overwhelming. Then Chapter 8, Riding Your Emotions, tells us all about dialectical behaviour therapy and ways to manage our emotions through specific skills that can help to make distress more manageable. Chapter 9, Coping in a Crisis, also uses evidence-based techniques from dialectical behaviour therapy to help when you're at breaking point. Finally, in Chapter 10, Being a Wise Owl, we use ideas from compassion-focused therapy and dialectical behaviour therapy to approach our decisions, thought processes and the impact of our emotions in a more balanced way.

In Part 3, we explore what kind of things can help us in our relationships. We think about how to better understand the minds of other people, how to say no, be assertive, and how to repair relationships. We also think a little about how to recognize if a relationship is becoming unhealthy, or even toxic. Chapter 11, Understanding the Minds of Others, talks about how we tune in and understand the unknowable – the inside of others – and how we can understand how we appear to others. It describes some of the traps you might fall into that can make relationships more difficult, and again returns to the idea of balance, being curious and being accepting of not just your own emotions, but of others' too. It also gives you techniques to help with this. Chapter 12 has some concrete skills building for being able to say no and be assertive (catchy title: Saying No and Being Assertive) because we know these are key skills that help you to get your needs met and have healthy, productive relationships.

Part 4 is pretty simple but really important. We talk about how you can approach getting extra help in Chapter 13 and we also list online resources, helplines and apps that we're reliably told are useful by professionals or young people we work with and trust. We finish up with Chapter 14 and the Self-Care Plan, which gives you a template to take all the bits you like and think are useful in the book so you can access and use them when you need them.

The appendices also contain a number of resources that will support you, linked to the different chapters.

That's about it. Now you can dive in and see what you think.

≳ Chapter 2 ≲

What's Wrong With Me?

So, if you struggle to manage big emotions, do you have a mental health problem? Are you mentally ill? Do you have some kind of disorder? It depends who you ask. It also depends on how often, how intensely, and whether it gets in the way of your studies (or paid work), friendships *and* family life.

One of the reasons we wanted to write this book is because managing emotions is a key skill that we have to *learn*. Adolescence (and we think of this as from 10 up to 25) is a time of great change, challenge and risk taking, so we're going to have times where we feel totally overwhelmed or out of control, and this is completely normal. We need to have the highs and the lows...we even need to be all over the place sometimes. This is how we learn about ourselves, our emotions, and find adult ways to cope with them. We learn how to ask for support and when to let the important people in our lives know what we need to help us feel OK. It's also important that we work out how our relationships are affected when we get overwhelmed by our feelings.

We start to learn about intense emotions and how to cope with them before we can even talk. It happens when we're babies and need adults to do everything for us. We cry or communicate with our faces and bodies, then our carers have to work out what we need to make us feel OK through playing, feeding, keeping us warm (or cooling us down) and soothing our distress. It's through adults helping us feel OK (the fancy word is 'co-regulation') that we learn that what goes on *inside us* can be understood by others, and that emotions are normal and manageable. We can then use what they have shown us so we can calm and soothe ourselves when they're not around. We also learn that other people are able to cope with our feelings and can make us feel OK when we need them to, so we're more likely to reach out and get support (that co-regulation) when we need it.

Why is managing emotions harder for some than others?

We know that we all need to learn to manage our emotions, but it seems that it's easier for some people than others to experience and cope with intense emotions. Some of this is just biology and individual difference – humans come in varieties. If you're lucky enough to find it easy, you're likely to have a less reactive temperament; by this we mean you don't experience your emotions as intensely and you probably didn't react with as much fear to new things when you were a baby. The other thing you're likely to have had is less separation and loss and fewer difficult experiences in your life. If you've experienced difficult things but are still good at coping with your feelings, then this is probably because you had adults (or maybe older brothers or sisters) around you who were able to read you and tune in to your emotions when you were little and then help you deal with them (that co-regulation thing again). We know that adults who can tune in and read a child can help them recognize their emotions, give their emotions names, and then calm their emotions down (or pep them up) according to what they need to feel OK in their bodies. This tuning in means that if you had a lot of stress or trauma when you were little, the supportive adult can understand your responses and help you make sense of everything. If this is how you're supported when difficult things happen, then you learn how to manage intense emotions. This can mean that experiencing difficult stuff leads to you being *more in control* than those without stress and difficult experiences (psychologists call this post-traumatic growth). This experience of being understood and supported also means you're more likely to trust other people to help and support you when you need it in the future, and this support makes intense feelings less overwhelming.

The problem is that when babies and children are exposed to a lot of difficult, and even traumatic, experiences, often their parent or carer is too. This means that the parent is stressed out or maybe scared, so it's much harder for them to tune in to their baby/child and make them feel OK. Some parents are *amazing* and manage to be tuned in even when they're stressed, and some children are lucky enough to have a grandparent, foster carer, teacher or someone else who's stable and calm and can help them manage the feelings or confusion about what's going on in their lives. However, if you really struggle to manage your emotions, then there's a good chance that you had some stress in your early life. This could be something like a parent with health problems, violence in the home, someone in your house who drank too much alcohol or was using drugs which made them unpredictable and even scary. Because your carer was living this too, it's likely that they were unable to tune in and help you manage your emotions, even though they might have really wanted to or tried to.

It could be that you just had lots of carers and they were all quite different. Often this happens when children live outside their family or in the care system, and they move homes frequently. For many reasons beyond their control, families can struggle to keep their children living just with them and they end up staying with lots of different family members. We know that this lack of predictability and consistency can cause lots of problems in both managing emotions and relationships because we all need someone who just 'gets us', makes us feel OK, who can be around enough of the time. Without this special person/people, then there're going to be more intense emotions (loneliness, grief, anger), and understanding and managing these feelings alone is hard.

Neurodevelopmental differences and intense emotions

If you have a diagnosis of a developmental difference such as autistic spectrum condition (ASC), attention deficit and hyperactivity disorder (ADHD) or foetal alcohol spectrum disorder (FASD), then it may be that you find emotions more difficult to understand or to manage. This might be because you have different ways of processing all kinds of information (including social information or sensory input) or due to problems with impulse control. Simply being identified as 'different' or receiving a diagnosis and label can cause a lot of intense emotions. You might also struggle with something that is seen as crucial to managing them (e.g. being able to stop, think and not just react). Also, if you have specific learning problems, such as dyslexia, or memory problems due to a brain injury, this can have an impact on your stress/frustration and lead to more difficult emotions.

Personality versus mental disorder

We think it's important to understand some of the language of 'disorder' that you might hear within mental health services or when you google (or use any other available search engines) so we wanted to talk about some of the diagnoses associated with intense emotions.

Due to our experiences of being either a psychologist or a person who has struggled with intense emotions and has been labelled 'disordered' for this, we are clear about our position – we do not ourselves use the term 'disorder' when we're talking about intense emotions, crises and people coping in the best way they know how. We do understand, however, that some people find labels really helpful, and sometimes they are. For example, post-traumatic stress disorder (PTSD) often involves really intense emotions and there are a number of psychological treatments that are specifically known to help relieve the suffering of PTSD (see Chapter 13 on Getting Extra Help). In this situation, a diagnosis can be really useful in getting the right help and in understanding where your emotions are coming from.

In the past, mental health professionals have talked about people who struggle to manage their feelings and relationships as having 'personality disorders'. This was seen as different from mental illness, because rather than 'symptoms', they described repeated patterns of behaviour that were considered to be unhelpful or even 'dysfunctional'. Rather than using the term 'dysfunctional', we prefer to think of these behaviours as being a way to survive when you were little. But when they stick around into adolescence and adulthood, they can cause problems in relationships, work life and functioning, because they no longer fit with the environment you're living in and the expectations of adulthood. Mental illnesses, however, would be thought of as being a set of symptoms that can happen at any time and are, for the most part, temporary, for example depression or panic disorder. Psychiatrists would often treat symptoms of mental illness through medication and psychologists through therapy (see Appendix II for a brief guide on medication for intense emotions). Initially, there was a belief that personality difficulties couldn't be treated because medication was not working. However, as they have been better understood as a way of coping with difficult early environments and relationships, a number of therapies have been applied successfully and new ones developed that specifically tackle the problematic patterns in relationships and ways of coping that would be described or diagnosed as a 'personality disorder'.

What specific diagnosis relates to intense emotions?

In the past within the Western world, women who showed problems with managing their emotions were labelled as 'hysterical'. This was a time when women had very little power so they had to keep secret a lot of the things that were causing them to feel sad, angry or overwhelmed. The label of 'borderline personality disorder' (BPD) was first used in the late 1970s to describe people (mainly women) who were struggling to manage emotions and relationships, and using destructive coping strategies such as self-injury, aggression or substances to deal with their distress. The term 'emotionally unstable personality disorder' (EUPD) is more commonly used in mental health services in the UK, but it describes the same kind of experiences.

DIAGNOSTIC DESCRIPTIONS OF BPD OR EUPD

☆ A personality disorder marked by a pattern of instability of interpersonal relationships, self-image and affects, and impulsivity, beginning by early adulthood and present in a variety of contexts.

☆ A serious mental illness marked by unstable moods and impulsive behaviour. People with BPD have problems with relationships, family and work life, long-term planning and self-identity. Symptoms include intense bouts of anger, depression and anxiety that may lead to self-injury or suicide, drug or alcohol abuse, excessive spending, binge eating or risky sex.

☆ Severe personality disorder that develops in early childhood, characterized by a lack of control of anger, intense and frequent mood changes, impulsive acts, disturbed interpersonal relationships, and life-threatening behaviours.

The above are descriptions of an extreme inability to manage relationships and emotions. Maybe you're thinking, 'This is me!' or maybe you're thinking, 'I'm reading the wrong book'. Stick with us.

If you have experienced a lot of trauma and not had the support to find ways to manage the feelings this has brought up, then self-injury and other risky behaviours can be the only way that you feel able to cope with your emotions. These behaviours are what usually lead to receiving a diagnosis. Guidance about using personality disorder as a diagnosis says clearly that these labels need to be treated with extreme caution when applied to young people. The term 'emerging personality disorder' is sometimes used for young people. We don't support the use of this term because we know that when a person seeks support from a mental health service, they're usually in crisis and reacting to their environment (what is happening around them). We would argue that it's nearly always not 'pervasive and enduring' when it happens in adolescence, because it's not been going on for long enough and at that age the young person is still very much developing (see Chapter 3 for information about our brain development), and learning who they are, how to cope in a crisis and how to manage their relationships. For a young person, it can also be harder to get away from the environments or people that are causing the distress. It might be difficult to think about, but actually destructive behaviour can sometimes make a lot of sense and be a way of coping with unspeakable and traumatic things. It's important for us to think about *the environment* a person is living in or has grown up in, *what experiences are behind extreme emotions* and *why* destructive behaviours are the way that a person copes with them.

Personality and neurodevelopment

We know that young people, particularly young women where the diagnosis of neurodevelopmental differences like autistic spectrum disorder may not have been picked up as easily as in young men, sometimes wrongly get a diagnosis of being 'emotionally unstable'. This can be especially unhelpful because this label can overshadow their social communication needs and mean that they don't receive the most helpful advice and support (and neither do their families). Sometimes young people try to 'mask' their social communication difficulties by trying hard to fit in and copying what the people around them are doing. This can be very tough and stressful, as it's hard to work out what you need to do to meet the expectations of others. Alongside this stress, young people with neurodevelopmental differences can often experience their senses much more strongly, which can feel too much. For example, being very sensory sensitive and struggling to integrate lots of different sensory information means that it is easy to become overwhelmed and struggle to regulate your emotions effectively. For young people with a diagnosis of autistic spectrum disorder or ADHD, there can be additional diagnoses around managing emotions, such as BPD or EUPD. We sadly acknowledge that young people who are not neurotypical are more at risk of bullying and prejudice and can be vulnerable to traumatic experiences in their early lives. We will go on to talk a lot about the impact of traumatic experiences on our emotions and how we handle them. Readers who have received a diagnosis of autistic spectrum disorder, ADHD or other developmental differences are just as, if not more, likely to have these experiences and the intense emotions they bring, with the possibility of less support to deal with them.

DR TURLOUGH MILLS, A CONSULTANT PSYCHIATRIST, TALKS ABOUT BORDERLINE PERSONALITY DISORDER

Disorders of personality development are not mental illnesses. They can be considered as adaptive, even protective, responses of the developing self/personality to experiences of trauma and adversity and to an absence of an emotionally validating care environment.

Characteristic features of BPD usually emerge in adolescence. Clinicians sometimes struggle to distinguish these from 'normal' features of adolescence, which might include, for example, mood swings, an unstable sense of self or identity, and tempestuous interpersonal relationships. Clinicians have also been anxious not to burden young people with a label that has carried a historical stigma of being perceived to be untreatable. This has led to an overall reluctance within child and adolescent mental health services (CAMHS) to have open and transparent discussions with young people about personality disorder and BPD, and in particular for professionals to use this diagnosis in the CAMHS population. This reluctance to discuss and diagnose BPD has clearly been a barrier to those young people who do meet the criteria for a diagnosis of BPD being able to access appropriate and effective care. In my experience as a CAMHS inpatient consultant, it has probably also contributed to young people having unnecessary and unhelpful hospital admissions.

As discussed extensively in this guide, a diagnosis of BPD is only helpful in the context of a formulation. A BPD formulation is likely to include past experiences of trauma, inconsistent or unpredictable caregiving environments and a lack of consistent emotional validation. The formulation is an effective tool to help young people and those around them (both caregivers and professionals) towards a more enriched understanding of how they are 'in the now' and how they have come to be the individuals that they are. A formulation also recognizes the dynamic nature of personality development: our personalities are formed over time, through a complex interplay of internal and external factors. The quality of our early relationships with those who care for us is of particular importance, as is the temperament that we are born with. These early relationships, which are often called attachments, form a blueprint for how we will go on to make relationships in childhood, adolescence, adulthood, with our own children and so on.

If we are looked after by people who consistently keep us safe, who are in tune with our needs and emotions and who make us feel loved and loveable, then it is likely that we will grow into someone who can trust others, who can tolerate frustrations and upsets and who feels, by and large, good about themselves. However, if the people who are supposed to be looking after us do not keep us safe, are not attuned to our emotional needs and do not help us to feel loved, then there is a significant risk that we might internalize a deeply held sense of ourselves as unloveable, even dangerous or poisonous, and see others as also dangerous and unreliable. This can lead people into very destructive behaviours, particularly in relation to others, and often as a reaction to feeling abandoned and betrayed. People can also struggle with intense feelings of self-hatred and may use self-harm or suicidal acts to try to kill off hated parts of themselves. These behaviours tend to reinforce relationship difficulties, which in turn fuel negative internal representations of the self.

BPD is characterized by internal factors (particular patterns of thinking and feeling) and external behaviours (emotional outbursts, relationship difficulties and self-harm). These patterns of thinking and feeling and the behaviours associated with them are normal responses to experiences of trauma and emotional invalidation, and all human beings will, at various points in their lives, feel these things. A diagnosis of BPD might need to be considered when these thoughts, feelings and behaviours have become predominant for a person and are significantly affecting that person's ability to function.

In BPD, it is usually maladaptive behaviours (e.g. self-harm) that most negatively affect functioning, including triggering hospital admissions. If behaviours can be managed, then functioning can be restored; but once functioning is restored, can this person still really be considered to have BPD?

Most treatment aims at reducing maladaptive behaviours. This is usually key in promoting better relationships, which in turn can help challenge negative internal representations of self. The most effective treatment is psychological (as detailed elsewhere in this guide).

So why would anyone want a diagnosis?

We understand that for some people whose feelings are unpredictable, running their lives and making them utterly miserable, there may be a huge sense of relief and some validation from a diagnosis. It makes it something you can tackle! Our worry is that it can also suggest that there is something 'wrong' with a person and ignore that they're simply coping with difficult environments, experiences or traumas. At its worse, it means that the things that are hurting a young person are not dealt with as instead *they* are seen as 'the problem'.

We would also argue that young people are more likely to show the 'symptoms' of EUPD as a part of their normal development, and the ups and downs we all go through as an adolescent and young adult. We talk in Chapter 3 about your adolescent brain and how regulating feelings and stopping yourself taking risks can be much harder for young people. If it's just normal developmental stuff, then we worry that the label can make you feel hopeless and become a self-fulfilling prophecy. Where it's seen over a period of years rather than months, it's often in response to difficult or traumatic things that the young person is experiencing or the way that adults are responding to their distress. We've seen lots of young people who appear 'disordered' but then when they move to a new school or home, or just find that person who really 'gets it' and makes them feel seen and safe, then they're much more able to manage their intense emotions. They were never the problem – it was their environment and lack of co-regulation and support.

Developmental trauma or 'complex PTSD'

When we meet young people who are struggling with intense emotions, they often say that they haven't experienced 'trauma' because they think this means seeing one terrible thing happen like a

WHAT'S WRONG WITH ME?

car crash, or being hurt by someone. Actually, when we're growing up there are other things that professionals now consider 'trauma' that might surprise you. Doctors, teachers and health professionals talk and think a lot now about adverse childhood experiences (ACEs). ACEs, despite their name, are definitely not good. We also think about benevolent childhood experiences (BCEs) that *are* actually ace. Totally confusing.

EXAMPLES OF ADVERSE CHILDHOOD EXPERIENCES (ACES)

☆ Parental separation

☆ Parent in prison

☆ Parent in hospital

☆ Seeing violence and conflict at home

☆ Parent with mental health problems (including postnatal depression)

☆ Being homeless

☆ Being called names, or criticized, by your parent

☆ Not having enough to eat or drink

☆ Feeling that you don't have a person whom you can go to when you need help

There are also more obvious traumas like being hit or hurt by your carers and being sexually abused that are big ACEs. But developmental trauma is a way that we now talk about what we know can be the long-lasting effects of difficult childhood experiences on your health and how you cope with not only your emotions, but your relationships and everyday stresses.

It's really important that if you've experienced any of these ACEs you remember they don't determine who you are or your future. For many people, they experience 'post-traumatic growth' which is what happens when your story is heard, your feelings understood and you become more able to cope with future stressors and can see yourself as resilient and strong. We now know that BCEs are the things that can make the difference and heal the harm and hurt of developmental trauma.

BENEVOLENT CHILDHOOD EXPERIENCES (BCES)

☆ Having at least one caregiver with whom you felt safe

☆ Having at least one good friend

☆ Having beliefs that give you comfort (e.g. in a god, or hope for the future)

☆ Enjoying school

☆ Having at least one teacher who cared about you

☆ Having good neighbours

☆ Having an adult who was not a parent/caregiver who could provide you with support or advice

☆ Having opportunities to have fun

☆ Liking yourself and/or feeling comfortable with yourself

☆ Having a predictable home routine with regular meals and a regular bedtime

So, you might be wondering, why are we talking so much about trauma? We think it's important to talk about it because we know from lots of research over people's lifespans, that people who struggle with intense emotions have had significant ACEs and a lack of BCEs. Research has also told us that 93 per cent of those with a diagnosis of EUPD have experienced this kind of early trauma. This doesn't mean we think that every young person who is struggling with emotions has experienced trauma, but we think the idea of asking, 'What happened to you?' is much more helpful and important than asking, 'What's wrong with you?'

Formulation

When we are working with young people who are really struggling to manage intense emotions, we try to understand where the big feelings come from, and what's in the environment that might be making you feel so angry, sad, unsafe or scared. This means that we don't treat 'symptoms' when we need to get the young person out of a scary or traumatic environment or relationship. There is often some 'core pain' or 'key fears' that drive your coping strategies. We talk about 'coping in the best way you know how' because we really believe that even behaviours that might be defined as dysfunctional or self-destructive are usually just people trying to feel safe and OK in their bodies and manage relationships, even if only for a short time. But often these strategies can have unintended consequences, which can sometimes lead to you feeling even worse about yourself or others.

This process of telling a story to try to find the best way to help is what psychologists call 'formulation'. Other people might call it, 'My story'. We think that trying to make sense of your feelings and coping strategies in this way can be the best place to start to make a plan for how to manage intense emotions and get the most out of your relationships. It doesn't discount the fact that biologically we are all different and some people will simply experience their emotions more intensely. But it does mean that we can be thoughtful and compassionate about where our coping strategies come from, and we can use these stories to find new more helpful ways to manage our feelings. We can also use them to help the people around us to understand some of our responses and how they might be able to help.

What's happened to you?

The first step of understanding is to think about difficult experiences that might have triggered your intense emotions in the past. We understand this can be hard to do. It might be things that happened when you were really little (e.g. domestic violence or losing someone you loved), things that happened in childhood (e.g. being criticized a lot by a parent/carer, receiving a diagnosis of autistic spectrum disorder or ADHD) or in adolescence (e.g. bullying, school exclusions, bereavement). It can be useful to think about relationships and when they have been tough, difficult experiences at school, and then any difficult experiences at work.

What am I really scared of?

If you can work out what core pain you're trying to avoid or protect yourself from, this can help you to understand your coping strategies and what imagined threat (that you're really fearful of happening) they're helping you to avoid or reduce. This is about figuring out how the things that have happened to you have shaped what you are concerned about, or even scared of, in the here and now. For example, often if you have experienced a lot of loss or moving around then the key fear might be that people will leave you and you will end up abandoned and alone. This fear can often be easily activated – maybe by goodbyes or if your partner didn't put their usual kiss at the end of their message. If you've been bullied at school then the key fear or concern might be that other people are going to criticize, reject or humiliate you – this fear could be triggered by something as simple as a funny look or passing comment.

It's crucial to think about both the external fears (such as others hurting or leaving you) and internal fears (like being overwhelmed by your feelings or difficult memories) as they're both important 'threats' that you will cope with in different ways.

Coping in the best way I know how...

Depending on your experiences and the key fears that these have left you with, you'll have found ways to avoid these threats and feel OK when they're overwhelming. It might be that you use eating lots of sweet food, drinking alcohol or smoking cigarettes to try to manage or avoid intense feelings, or that you push people away when they get close to avoid the pain of them rejecting you. You may isolate yourself and be aloof, so you don't have to worry about putting your trust in other people. It could be that you cope with your fear of not being good enough by constantly striving to be the best and 'perfect' in your relationships and work.

SOME COMMON COPING STRATEGIES

☆ Avoidance – this can be of relationships, feelings and trying new things

☆ Always being on the look-out for danger, threat and rejection (hypervigilance)

☆ Keeping your head down, not asserting yourself and not making a fuss (being passive)

☆ Trying to please, accommodate and maintain relationships at any cost

☆ Striving to be perfect/achieve

☆ Not trying at all for fear of failing

☆ Being really hard on yourself (self-criticism)

- ☆ Trying to ignore difficult feelings/memories (suppression)

- ☆ Blocking out difficult feelings/memories using drugs/alcohol/self-harming

- ☆ Relying on yourself and no one else

- ☆ Seeking reassurance from others

When you're thinking about coping strategies that you might use, it can be useful to have someone who knows you well to help you think about it. When you've been using a strategy for a long time it can be hard to see where it comes from or link it to your fears as it just becomes 'what you do'. Remember that if you tend to be self-critical (perhaps as a way of protecting yourself), this can make it even more difficult when you're looking at how you cope. Be aware of any 'should' or 'should nots' creeping in. You need to be able to recognize and be compassionate about these as they are understandable responses to dealing with your fears and are just you coping in the best way you know how.

Unintended consequences

We are pretty clear that these coping strategies made sense at some point in your lives and also often make you feel better right away. For example, if you tell the person you really like that you don't want to hang out with them again, then you might feel an initial flood of relief that you don't have to tolerate the anxiety of waiting and expecting them to reject you. But over time you might start to feel sad about missing them and even angry with yourself for not giving them (and you) a chance at the relationship developing.

If you start to feel angry because a friend really let you down and then choose to suppress it, ignore it and be passive so as not to upset your friend, then you don't have to deal with the anger or difficult interaction. But then they do it *again*. Now you're twice as angry at them and also angry at yourself. These are the unintended consequences.

Sometimes coping strategies work well at avoiding the feared outcome, but they also reinforce the unhelpful ideas we have about ourselves, other people and the world and keep us trapped in the same patterns of behaviour and the same kinds of relationships. For example, if you push people away to keep yourself safe, then you will undoubtedly have fewer people in your life and so the ideas, 'I am not loveable' and, 'Other people are not there for me' are strengthened and there are even more reasons to hide away...and you're stuck in a vicious cycle.

Protective factors

The things that make us feel good, alive and connected are often key to learning to manage intense emotions, so it's important to spend some time reflecting on and recording what exactly these things are. They could be personal qualities (e.g. I can laugh at myself) or they might be activities that you enjoy (e.g. yoga or playing football). Again, asking for help from a key adult or friend can help, as can simply asking yourself, 'What would [insert name of favourite friend/carer/teacher] say has kept me strong and what would they recognize as my best qualities?'

You can find a template for writing your formulation in the appendices and we hope that this helps you to try to move away from, 'What is wrong with me?' to thinking about, 'What has happened to me? And how has this made me feel and then shaped how I am coping with my feelings now?' This provides you with a good starting point for working out what is going to help and what strategies you can try to feel more in control of your feelings and happier in your relationships.

JADE'S STORY

Throughout my experience with mental health services, both NHS and voluntary, from about the age of 11, I never once went through a formulation or 'my story' with the community mental health service. Their main focus seemed to be trying to give me a diagnosis. They gave me the label 'PTSD' without really knowing what was causing the symptoms for it. They were trying to help someone without a clear understanding of how they could help me. I believe you can have five people in a room with PTSD who all have very different traumas which need to be treated in very different ways. There are so many different ways to help people with trauma so instead of constantly going through a big list of therapies, with a formulation the people working to help you can narrow down what they may need to do. Trauma can be caused by all sorts – you have your big traumas and your little traumas and everything adds up, every person will have different causes for their mental health. Every mental illness is very complex and caused by many different factors, so by not having the understanding of my formula or my story how could they know how to help me, what therapies, medication (if needed) and overall support I needed? I believe that the cause of me hitting so many brick walls and struggling so much to work with them while being under community child and adolescent mental health services was to do with them not having a formulation, not having a clear understanding of me as an individual.

When I got put into inpatient services that was the first time I'd ever done a formulation. I didn't even know what a formulation was until my psychologist sat down and explained it to me and I filled one out. I felt as if this allowed my main care team to understand and actually help me to understand why I suffer with the symptoms I do, instead of just having a label. After so long being so confused about how I was feeling and what I was doing, it was some sort of explanation, which I believed benefited me a lot. Also, I believe it gave me the best shot at some of the therapies I tried, even though I didn't complete them because I wasn't quite ready. This understanding meant that my psychologist could find the therapies that were right for me, and they were actually trying to help me deal with the things I struggled with.

Within my formulation, my psychologist and I also did a trauma umbrella. I had never done one of these before. It helped me understand how PTSD can cause other symptoms from other mental illnesses. I was shocked when I did this because I didn't know this stuff before. People believe trauma is just flashbacks and nightmares when in fact there is so, so much more, for example hearing voices, seeing things, feeling depressed, dissociation, intrusive thoughts and many more symptoms. To this day, I have my trauma umbrella up on my wall.

I truly believe that every professional working with a person with mental health difficulties should do a formulation with the person.

Bringing it all together

Having read this chapter, some of you may be thinking you have a serious disorder, others may be feeling a bit sad from thinking about difficult things, or you may be wondering if you need to read on. We know that this isn't an easy start to the book. We also think that the ideas and strategies we talk about are not just for people who have experienced difficult stuff but are useful for all young people trying to work out how to become healthy adults. We wanted to think about what lies behind intense emotions and we think it's helpful for you to do this too, but maybe you need to take some time out to take care of yourself, have a treat, or wrap yourself up in a blanket (read Chapter 7 for some more good ideas!). Looking after yourself, especially when reflecting on your emotions and relationships, is really important, and we hope that you will learn more ways to do this using this book.

⋛ Chapter 3 ⋚

Understanding Your Brain

Chapter 2 talked about how our early life experiences, and how we are supported through them, can impact on our ability to cope with intense emotions. This chapter throws one more important thing into the mix: our brain development. You might be thinking, why is there a chapter in here about brains? That sounds too scientific and too much like homework (which is also what Sue thought when she started writing this chapter...but then she changed her mind... honest). But we would argue that *this* is what you should be learning in college and university, as it's all about you and what is going on in your brain right now and how this impacts on your emotions, risk taking and relationships. There are so many complex, important processes which are going to make such a big difference in your development over the next few years and into your mid-20s. Your brain is currently having a complete renovation, in order to become a more efficient, smoother running, faster machine. There are going to be some glitches on the way, which we will explore in this chapter, but the outcome will be amazing.

This chapter will focus on what the brain changes in adolescence (age 10–25 approximately) are, and the ways that they can affect us. It will show that although we do have choices in what we do, there are serious underlying biological reasons for some of our behaviours. We are stuck with some parts of our brains not yet fully working, but also being the subject of intense electrical activity and change, which means that sometimes when we need them to be working at their best, they're busy doing something else (i.e. developing neurobiologically). You might notice as you read through this chapter that some of the normal developmental tasks sound familiar, and in some ways mirror some of the 'symptoms' that were discussed in Chapter 2. This is therefore another reason why we need to apply caution when thinking about the use of diagnosis, or thinking that there is something 'wrong' with people, when they are going through so much change.

EXTRACT FROM BRAINSTORM

You say to me
Your brain is broken
It's like an adult brain, but it doesn't work properly.

You say
When you become a teenager, something happens.
Your brain shrinks or something.
It stops working properly.
You get so full of thinking about yourself that you forget about anyone else.

I say
When I'm wild and out of control
It's because I'm finding out who I am
What the world is
All the things I might be

And if I was a real wild animal
Then I'd have left by now.
But I haven't.
And I'm not going to. Yet.

I say
My brain isn't broken
It's like this for a reason
I'm becoming who I am
And I'm scared
And you're scared
Because who I am might not be who you want me to be
Or who you are.

Excerpt from *Brainstorm*, copyright © 2016 by Ned Glasier, Emily Lim and Company Three, reprinted with permission of the publishers, Nick Hern Books: www.nickhernbooks.co.uk

What you might also find is that a lot of people in your life, including parents/carers and even tutors, might not be aware of what we will talk about in this chapter. This is pretty new and ground-breaking stuff. Before the late 1990s, people (including scientists) used to believe that the human brain stopped developing when we reached mid-childhood. However, in the late 1990s, brain scans showed us that during adolescence lots of important changes happen in the brain and they restructure it and help it to be more efficient. These brain changes carry on until our mid-20s. Also, although we used to think that the big changes in the brain (plasticity) stopped after this time in life, evidence is really clear now that adaptations and changes keep happening through our whole lives. So even though the structure of your brain might not change at the same rate as it does during your teenage years, all brains can get better at what they do, even in adults.

Remodelling your brain

Your brain is currently being remodelled and developed, to be the best that it can be. What we know is that we are born with quite big brains (babies' heads are quite big in comparison with their bodies) and our brains keep growing until the age of eight or nine years, when they're adult size. However, the make-up of your brain then changes. The amount of grey matter (the squishy, grey tissue on the surface of the brain) starts to decrease from late childhood and into your mid-20s (you lose approximately 1.5 per cent of your grey matter per year). At the same time, the white matter (which is the inner communication centres of the brain), starts to increase by about 1 per cent per year.

So, during adolescence there are three main processes that happen, that change your brain structure to make it more effective, streamlined and much, much faster at processing information. Your brain when you're a child and teenager can learn and grow at an incredible rate. It's like a jack of all trades that can turn its hand to anything. As it becomes an adult brain, it starts to specialize in more specific tasks that it knows well and becomes a 'master craftsman'. Your brain is truly amazing.

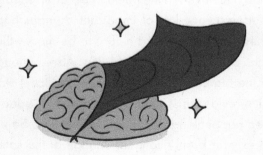

BRAIN CHANGES DURING ADOLESCENCE

Process 1: Pruning

Your brain contains about 86 billion neurons (brain cells) – this number stays about the same throughout your life (although some do die, and some are newly generated) – but the number of synapses (connections between neurons) changes. During childhood, our brains are like sponges and we soak in all the knowledge we can from our environment (learning everything about everything), so we over-produce connections between brain cells. You can imagine this like a growing tree, but it soon gets overgrown and unruly. So, as we become an adolescent, our brains start to prune themselves to cut back the unruly branches (the connections that we no longer use), so that our brain can become more specialized. We call this 'use it or lose it' – if you don't use that connection, the brain will automatically prune that bit out. But, if you use that connection on a regular basis, the brain will continue to grow and strengthen those connections. So, our brains are very sensitive to our environments, constantly getting feedback from what we are exposed to, and what we use in our everyday lives.

Process 2: Axon growth

Axons are the long fibres in the white (inner) bit of the brain that transmit electrical impulses around the brain and connect the different areas. During adolescence, they start to lengthen and widen, which means that the speed in which they can transmit the impulses increases, making them quicker and more connected.

Process 3: Linking the brain together

The axons also start to get coated in a white substance called 'myelin'. Although this might sound a bit disgusting, it's actually very clever. It's a bit like getting high-speed fibre broadband, as the myelin massively speeds up the transmission of the electrical impulses (communications) across the brain. So much so, that the transmission becomes 100 times quicker than before, and the resting period between transmissions is 30 times shorter. So, in total, your brain cells are able to communicate 3000 times faster than before! Myelin is a bit like an insulator, as it stops the electricity going anywhere other than where it's supposed to and prevents the 'wires touching', which could lead to confusion!

So, we now know what is happening to your brain during adolescence, but now let's think about how it might affect you day to day and explain some of your behaviour.

I will need more sleep

You might find that your parent or partner is constantly moaning about you lying in bed until lunchtime at weekends or struggling to get out of bed during the week. But these different sleeping patterns are completely normal for young people. The changes that you're going through in your brain will make it much harder to get to sleep initially, and often young people will only start to get sleepy around 1am (rather than the 10pm bedtimes other people may prefer). Also, as your brain is constantly developing and being built, it needs more sleep. In fact, the recommended sleep for teenagers is 8–11 hours per night (compared with the 7–9 hours recommended for adults). So, there's a biological basis that you'll be wanting to stay up late and will need to stay in bed longer in the mornings so that your brain gets enough sleep. See Chapter 6 for more information about how to make sure that you're getting enough, and good quality, sleep.

I can't always manage my emotions, they will sometimes be too big

As you're going through adolescence, the part of your brain which helps you to control and manage your emotions (the prefrontal cortex just behind the forehead) is slowly developing, but it won't be fully developed until you're in your mid-20s. Your brain develops at different rates. The parts of your brain that create emotional responses develop quickly, so they're fully developed through most of your teenage years. This means that you have strong emotional reactions to things, which can lead to meltdowns, where you suddenly feel angry, sad, scared or upset. Similarly, you can feel strong positive emotions such as joy, excitement, passion and giddiness. But, when you feel such strong emotions, the parts of the brain that you need to calm them down aren't fully developed yet. So, you have the strong emotions, but can't manage them. It's a bit like building a car and putting in the engine before you give it any brakes or a steering wheel; the power is there, but you don't have the ability to control it or stop the car when needed – it just has to come to a stop on its own.

It's important for me to take more risks

Sometimes, or maybe often, you might find that older people around you say that you make 'silly' decisions. Or they might say, 'Why did you do that?' When we're in our teens or early 20s, we are governed by different 'drives' from adults. During adolescence, we tend to have an increased desire for rewards, to seek out new and exciting experiences and take risks, which are important for our development. Dopamine is a chemical in our brains which is known to motivate us to seek a reward and can give us a bit of a rush when we get there. As the dopamine level is generally lower in our brains during adolescence, this can lead to us generally feeling more bored. However, when we do something that we find risky or exciting, we can get a dopamine 'rush' or buzz. This might mean that we end up more focused on the thrill or reward that we get for doing something and will ignore potential risks or challenges because nothing is worse than feeling nothing.

The prefrontal cortex that helps with managing emotions is also involved in a range of complex skills like decision making, putting a stop to inappropriate behaviours and impulses, being able to think about how we look and are understood by other people and how we get along and understand others. It's also a critical part of the brain to help us effectively plan, such as planning what you're going to do tonight, tomorrow and five years from now. The prefrontal cortex is also a bit like a brake, which can help us to pause, hesitate, reflect and wonder. Without it, we would say the first thing that came into our head all the time. In adolescence, the emotional and chemical surges that we experience can mean that all the random stray thoughts that we have can just tumble out of our mouths before we can stop them. Afterwards we might think, 'Oops, I shouldn't have said that!' Imagine what the world would be like if we always said the first thing that came into our heads... (scary). So, our prefrontal cortex helps us to have space to look at the world and what we see from different perspectives and make sense of the behaviour of ourselves and others. However, this part of the brain is still developing, so sometimes we will feel emotions or desires strongly, but won't have the brake to make us pause or reflect before taking a risk.

So, if the system that gives you a kick out of risk taking is developed before the system that inhibits risk taking, then that will increase the likelihood that you will take risks. The good thing about this change is that it can encourage us to try new things and enjoy life more. It can also be good to take risks, as it's part of our development. We need to get out in the world and make our way, and we often learn from trial and error. But sometimes we can see the thrill and reward that we could get from something but forget about the risk (or not see it as important). So, this means that we can end up being quite impulsive – doing things for the thrill, but not thinking them through fully, not thinking about what could potentially go wrong. For example, if you ask your parent/carer to get on a big horse, they might be more likely to think about the potential for them to fall off and hurt themselves, and how far from the ground they might be. A younger person might think more about how fun it might be. When Sue was a teen (such a long time ago), she would sometimes walk home from a party by herself in the dark. At the time, she just was feeling happy from being at the party, and tired and wanting to get home. Although she was aware of the potential risks, they just didn't seem important to her at the time. Now, with her (so much) older adult brain, she would never walk alone in the dark as she is too aware of the risks (but then again, she's less likely to be staying out late at a party too...).

My friends are going to be very important to me

You might find that as you get older, you want to spend less time with your parents/carers and more with your friends. This is totally normal. You might also find that you think that the views of people your age are *far* more important than adults' – I mean, what do they really know? This is also completely normal. As adolescents, we automatically start to spend more time with people our age, and this is a healthy transition in a lot of ways as we start on a long journey to becoming more independent. Good peer relationships are important for our overall wellbeing and happiness. However, you might have heard of the term 'peer influence'. This is usually used in a negative way and is about how, when we are with people our age, and don't care about adult advice, we can sometimes get involved in taking risks or making decisions that are completely fuelled by our adolescent brains, which can make us be impulsive, chase after a thrill and not even think about the consequences (or not see them as important at the time). Sometimes we might do things when we are with our friends that we wouldn't dream of doing on our own, such as making mean jokes about other people. We sometimes do this when we get caught up in having fun with friends, and their laughter makes us feel good and want to do it more. Similarly, we might find ourselves being talked into things like going on rollercoasters or bungee jumping, which we wouldn't ordinarily do. There are lots of research studies that focus on peer influence. For example, a 2005 study by Margo Gardner and Laurence Steinberg watched young people playing computer games. When they played the games with their friends standing behind them, they took three times the number of risks than they did when they were playing alone. This has also been shown to happen with car journeys, where young people are more likely to have accidents, particularly when they have people of a similar age in the car with them (which is why your car insurance will probably be really expensive!). Perhaps strangely, this also occurs in mice, where adolescent mice have been found to drink more alcohol when they're with other mice than when they're on their own! The same thing doesn't happen with the grown-up mice, as researchers led by Sheree Logue showed in 2014.

It's therefore known that young people can often make different decisions, and take more risks, when they're with their friends than when they're on their own. This happens at all ages (adults do it too!) but adolescents are particularly susceptible. This is a period of life when you start to develop your identity, who you are, and the views of others (especially other young people your age) might feel particularly important. As teens, we become very worried about being excluded by friends or other young people. So sometimes it can feel easier, or better, to take a risk in order to fit in. So, although sometimes to someone else your behaviour may seem nonsensical, there might be a clear rational reason for it. For example, it might feel riskier to potentially be excluded by your peer group for not taking an illegal drug, rather than trying one. This is not just specific to young people though, as we are all influenced by how we think other people might see us, but for young people, being accepted in their peer group is their most important 'task'.

Impact of trauma on the developing brain

We know that during childhood and the teenage years, our brains are going through critical developmental periods and are particularly sensitive to the impact of the environment around us (where we live, what we have been through, our relationships, etc.). For young people who have had early difficult experiences, all the adolescent changes of wanting to be part of a group, taking more risks, making poor decisions, being impulsive, can lead to more intense emotions and then unhelpful coping strategies seeming 'normal' and being valued by the peer group.

Risk taking, feeling lost, struggling to find your identity are going to feel more intense if you have experienced trauma. Trauma has a significant impact on our brain development, as the bits of the brain that deal with our survival response (fight/flight/freeze), such as the amygdala and brain stem, actually over-develop in young people who have had to live in difficult environments where they don't feel safe, meaning that they're neurologically hardwired to respond to potential threat. We sometimes call this the 'meerkat brain', where a person is hyper-aware of their surroundings and any potential threat, and easily triggered into their survival response. Their emotions may also feel more intense and may be more difficult to calm. But the brain is an amazing thing, and with the right kinds of help and support it can start to heal. So, starting to do things differently when you're a young person is good timing as we know that big changes are already taking place and if you practise using healthy coping strategies then these are the connections that survive. (So please stay away from *Candy Crush* as no one needs those synapses hardwired!)

Rebuilding your brain

So, as this chapter explains, your brain is currently being rebuilt. During its renovation, there are going to be a few glitches, but if you understand them and put up an extra bit of scaffolding (allow some support from those close to you), you're going to thrive. Difficulties with intense emotional responses, taking risks, being impulsive and needing more sleep can be normal and important parts of your development. However, they can also be difficult to get through, especially if you don't have support around you to help you to do this. So, the later chapters in this book will help you to learn strategies in order to look after yourself while you're still rapidly developing (and into the future).

Chapter 4

Big Emotions and Relationships: Loving So Much It Hurts

This chapter starts by thinking about how our relationships affect our ability to understand and manage intense emotions. It then goes on to think about a particular way of relating to other people called 'anxious attachment' that is related to struggling with big feelings. This type of relating is also sometimes called 'preoccupied' as it feels as if relating to others and being close to them is the only way to feel OK.

When people are struggling to manage big feelings, we know that they're often also struggling with their relationships. When we're overwhelmed by our feelings, it can be hard to read other people and work out what they're thinking and feeling (see Chapter 11), so we're not as able to relate to them. In this case, the big emotions can really contribute (and come before) the relationship difficulties.

Another reason that difficulties in relationships and big emotions come together is that the biggest hurt most of us face is being rejected by others or losing the people we love. Although our relationships are the source of love, comfort and support, they can also have the power to cause a lot of pain and suffering. Losing someone you love is often the most painful thing a person can experience, whether this is a bereavement or the end of a relationship. Experiencing separation and loss, the sort of relationships you had when you were little and/or are in right now, can mean you are more sensitive to rejection or abandonment and all the intense emotions that brings (see Chapter 2).

This chapter will focus on how your experience of relationships (and especially of being cared for when you were little) can affect not just the way that you experience and manage your emotions, but, importantly, how you relate to the people you love and your approach to future relationships.

How relationships teach us about emotions

We know that you learn about yourself and your emotions through your early relationships. The relationship with your parents or first carers (might be a grandparent, foster carer or nanny) is so important for helping you to understand and learn to manage feelings because when you are little you can't do it without help. Babies and toddlers rely on adults to read them and tune in to what they want, need and feel. They can't calm themselves down when they get over-excited or frustrated, they struggle to find stuff to do when they get bored, and they need the adults around them to help them feel OK in their bodies. They have no words for the different feelings and so they use the responses of the adults around them to understand their feelings and to learn how they should manage them. As children get older, the adults around them often start to give words to their emotions:

'You got really cross' or 'You're so excited!' This builds their emotional vocabulary and means they know that these things going on in their bodies are real and other people pay attention to them. It also teaches them that it's OK to have these emotions and that others will 'get it' and help them to manage them so they'll feel OK.

There's a lot of research that shows that adults who use lots of language to describe and talk about what's going on inside their child's mind (their thoughts, feelings, intentions), and don't just talk about the behaviours that they can see, have children who are more able to manage their feelings and have more secure relationships. So, we know that this is an important part of emotional development. This means that if we, for whatever reason, don't have an adult who can help us to understand our feelings, we are doubly struggling. We're going to have more difficult feelings (sad, scared, lonely, bored, wet, hungry) and these feelings are going to be more overwhelming because there's no one who can help us or show us how we can manage them and start to feel OK again. A psychologist called Jon Allen calls this the *double disability*.

Why relationships are crucial to learning how to manage intense emotions

We don't want to labour this point as it seems mean to take a pop at babies and toddlers, but they're really not much use at anything other than being exceptionally cute and getting adults to love them. All babies and toddlers are very loveable. So, when you were little, like all humans, you were completely relying on the adults around you to keep you alive. You couldn't feed yourself, keep yourself warm (or cool yourself down if you're living somewhere warm) or keep yourself clean. Sorry, but you were really hopeless without an adult around. As a toddler, you couldn't manage frustration or other feelings and needed an adult to make sense of your feelings and show you how to manage them. You needed to learn that emotions are OK, completely normal, and will pass. When people talk about the 'terrible twos', it's because at that age feelings are BIG and the ability to be reasonable and find ways to feel better is minimal (to none). Without a person who can work out your feelings and help you feel OK again, then emotions quickly get too big and you feel totally overwhelmed. The child has to try to find their own ways to make sure they feel OK. In this respect, little humans are incredibly smart because they can adapt to things not being great. They might just start to ignore their feelings, and cut off from their bodies (see Chapter 5), or they might do the same things again and again to get comfort, or be super noisy/adorable to make sure that someone sticks around close to them.

Are you saying that to learn about and manage emotions I need a perfect parent?

No. We are definitely not blaming parents for difficulties in understanding and managing emotions. No parent in the world can be perfectly tuned in and available all the time. Everyone will have experienced moments of feeling alone, lost, humiliated or rejected by the people who loved and cared for them. We then develop ways to cope with the difficult feelings that this brings up without it being terrible for how we feel about ourselves, other people or the world. We learn that other people don't get it sometimes or can get it really wrong, but that we can repair, and things will be OK again. These coping strategies might be annoying to the people who live with us, but they don't cause us too much trouble. Most importantly, we use what adults have taught us when they were tuned in so we can develop healthy ways to soothe ourselves when they're not able to do it, like saying positive things in our heads (e.g. 'You can do it!') or giving ourselves a hug, or just taking a minute to breathe deeply and look around for support. These kinds of strategies stop us relying on others to make us feel OK all the time. You probably do some of them without even realizing it. It's really important for our future relationships for us to know that we can cope alone and that even when the person is not physically there, they're thinking about us and we're thinking about them, and this kind of support is enough for a while.

LEARNING THAT BIG FEELINGS ARE OK – BRIDIE

My little girl is three and loves to be at home doing puzzles. She would rather be with her family than anywhere else and would often get really upset when she had to go to nursery, crying, shouting and kicking out. When she got upset, we would work hard to do deep breaths, take our time and stay calm, give her lots of cuddles (to help her calm the feelings in her body), and tell her that we knew the goodbye made her feel really sad (giving her words for the feelings), but that she was going to have loads of fun and we would be back after her afternoon sandwiches. This could sometimes be hard because the stress of being late for work made it more difficult to tune in to the feelings of sadness and not just see the behaviour of kicking out.

Using my own self-soothing strategies and support made this possible. Soon the crying stopped and although she is still hesitant sometimes, she takes a deep breath and tells herself (out loud!) that she is going to have loads of fun and Daddy will be back after the sandwiches. She has learned that the sad feeling is OK and that both she and the adults can deal with it and it will pass, so although she still feels a bit sad, we now don't see any of the shouting or crying and it feels manageable for everyone. At three, she is learning that big feelings are OK and that they don't stick around forever.

Co-regulation: How another person helps us feel OK

We know that animals quickly pick up on anxiety and stress in their families or groups, and then quickly feel calm when the other animals are calm. Think about rabbits in a field all nibbling away and then one hears a twig snap. That rabbit stops eating, pricks up his ears and stands still, tense and alert for danger. The interesting bit is that so do all the other rabbits, even though they didn't hear anything. They pick up on the tense watchful state of the rabbit straightaway. This keeps them all safe. As soon as the rabbit starts eating again and relaxes, so do all the other rabbits. This is what happens in human families too. When we see our parents can deal with stuff, we feel safe and are able to calm down too. This is called 'co-regulation'. The quickest way to calm down and deal with stress is to be close to people whom we trust and care about. A clever group of researchers led by Naomi Eisenberger in 2011 showed us that just holding hands with a stranger can help us feel less distressed by pain and deal with it better. So when we have someone who is calm and containing (recognizes how we feel, lets us know they recognize and understand, but also lets us know it's OK and manageable), then we can calm down more quickly and are less likely to feel overwhelmed by emotions.

Being 'clingy' or 'needy' – anxious attachment and intense emotions

So, what happens when the adults in our lives are not able (for whatever reason) to offer co-regulation or be consistent and predictable? Because little people are totally reliant on adults to help, if you don't have a tuned-in, predictable adult then you might feel that the *whole world* is unpredictable. If the adult gets overwhelmed by your feelings and can't contain them and help you calm down, then this can increase your distress and it can feel really unmanageable. This can lead to you feeling anxious and even unsafe, so it makes sense to cling to others and make sure that they're paying attention to you. You begin to focus on keeping them around to make you feel safe – 'I am OK if I'm with you' – but then it's not quite calming enough.

Feelings can be even more overwhelming and scary if they make adults angry, or mean they suddenly ignore us rather than tuning in and trying to help us understand and manage them. Sometimes at the end of a long day, it's really hard for a parent to stay calm when a tired child gets angry and upset about a small thing and the parent might show their frustration by shouting at them or walking away. This kind of 'not getting it' is normal, but if this reaction to intense emotions happens again and again, then the child learns that these feelings are bad and adults can't help them.

If adults aren't there when we need them enough of the time, then one way of adapting and coping is to do everything we can to try to keep them with us and caring for us when they're tuned in, because we don't feel OK when they're not around. We also have no opportunity to learn healthy ways to calm ourselves down or manage our emotions. This might mean that we have to exaggerate our emotions to make sure that they know that we need them to stay with us and make us feel OK. Little children will cry a lot when their parents leave them (totally normal). But for some children, even when their parent comes back, they keep being very upset, because they worry that if they don't keep crying then the parent will go away, they can't be sure how they will be when they do come back, and because they're more distressed at being left alone in the first place. When we're focused on just keeping adults close by, we aren't often able to find healthy ways to cope with the intense emotions that are coming up. In fact, for lots of children it might even be *unhelpful* to learn how to cope alone and show self-soothing skills, because what if the adult thinks we don't need them at all and we can cope alone?

Being 'clingy' or 'needy' are descriptions that almost no one would like to hear about themselves, but needing other people is absolutely part of being human. Needing an adult when you're a child is entirely normal and appropriate and even well into adolescence we need lots of support to get through the challenging stuff. We have a problem that in Western culture even young children can be described by parents and teachers as 'clingy', 'needy' or 'attention seeking', when actually they should be described as *attachment* or *care* seeking, which is exactly what we want children to do when they need support. This is how you learn how to ride the waves and when to get some help.

Loving a lot can't be a bad thing, right?

We understand that this way of approaching relationships makes a lot of sense to lots of people. If you're a young person who has not had a predictable adult who 'gets it' and taught you how to calm and soothe yourself, or you have experienced lots of rejection from family and/or peers, then it makes sense that you are anxious about relationships and losing people, so try to keep others close and thinking about you. You might feel that having a special person who can be there all the time is the answer to managing your intense emotions and feeling better. Other people's responses to your intense emotions might be something you think about a lot, and that both making sure that they understand how much you need them and keeping them happy must be prioritized. It makes sense for you to invest a lot of energy in making sure other people are going to stay close so that they're there when you need them. Sometimes people might behave like this temporarily, usually because of a lot of pressure or a crisis. However, if this is how most relationships feel, then it might be that you're acting out old ways of coping with not being sure there is someone there to make you feel OK, and that you've developed ideas about yourself and other people that keep these patterns going such as: 'I'm incapable and unable to cope alone', and 'Others are unpredictable and will reject me'. This can be when struggling with relationships and intense emotions becomes a bigger problem.

Does this sound familiar to you or does it remind you of someone close to you? It often means you do everything you can to please the other person, work out what you think they want and need, invest a lot of energy in becoming the perfect friend, partner or daughter/son and worry a lot about doing the right thing, concerned about when they decide they don't like you anymore. The other person may not be aware of how worried you feel, or they may see some of the anxiety. You feel OK when they're with you, but then worry a lot when they're doing other things. Or even when they are with you, you might find yourself worrying about when it's going to go wrong and when they will reject you or leave (as you perceive other people have done in the past). As time passes and they don't invest the same level of energy into the relationship, and/or struggle to respond to the feelings that you hide from them, then you feel hurt, abandoned and angry; you may even reject them and turn away from them. The other person is often then confused by these strong feelings as they don't see or understand where they come from.

LOVING SO MUCH IT HURTS: BEST FRIENDS

When I was 15, I got my first real 'best friend'. It was all I ever wanted. I always felt like the odd one out, even though I had lots of friends. We liked the same music, we loved singing, she was kind and funny. I should have been happy and on the surface I was. I loved having someone to be with all the time and felt excited to go to school and happy at the weekend when we were together. What was unbearable was when she was going to places where I couldn't (my parents are strict!) or even worse where I wasn't invited. I could not settle, I felt sick, I was imagining her finding someone she liked better or someone saying something mean about me and her realizing that I was not at all the kind of best friend she wanted. It meant that I was desperate to be at all the things she went to even if it was not really my bag and I felt awkward or out of place. It also meant that I was always asking her who she was with or what people had been saying about me. It took a while but slowly my worst fears came true and she started to look embarrassed when I was around, get irritated when I was asking her questions about what others were saying. I noticed that her other friends were saying I was weird or fancied her. They had noticed how intense I was and found it odd. Looking back now, I can see how my behaviour led to the end of the friendship, and even at the time I knew that my fear of losing her was making me behave strangely, but I just wasn't able to take a step back because the feelings were so intense.

Problematic attachment

If the fear of rejection is really strong, then the relationships can be even more difficult. If you actually believe 'I am unloveable' or 'I am not worthy of love' and 'Other people are untrustworthy', then you might only be able to keep others close by being someone completely different, hiding all your thoughts and feelings for fear of being 'seen' in all your badness and then rejected. You might make up stories to try to keep them close and to make sure they don't see any of the real hurts, and share a lot of negative feelings (anger and/or sadness) to make sure that they know that you really need them to stay close and they're the only one who can keep you safe and make you feel OK. This is a very intense relationship that may be satisfying to the other person for a while because they feel important and 'needed', but the intensity can become too much and the person begins to retreat or feel a lot of resentment. There might also be some heated arguments where you say things that you regret, because the intense emotions that come with your fear of abandonment get out of control (see Chapter 12 about when relationships can become unhealthy).

MARK'S STORY

When I was doing my A-levels, I met a girl who was super smart, funny and interesting and I could not believe she wanted to go out with someone as ordinary and boring as me. She was quite moody and could be distant at times, which made me feel a bit worried about us, but then she would want to spend lots of time together too and would send me these emails and messages telling me how important I was and that she couldn't live without me. I felt as if I was being pushed away only to be pulled back in. Sometimes there were tests – she would not call for days and then turn up at my house furious saying that I did not care about her because I hadn't tried to call or message her enough times (even though I had sent a text or message and tried to call at least once each day). I started to feel exhausted from all the pushing and pulling. I still really liked her, but I was fed up of not knowing whether I was the problem or the solution! I tried to end the relationship, but she said she couldn't live without me and she would do something drastic, so I felt too scared and didn't. When I told my mum about this, she was very worried about both my girlfriend and me. She helped me to see that this was not healthy and that I needed get out of the relationship and let my girlfriend's parents know that she was having a hard time and required more support, so I didn't feel so guilty. I still think about her sometimes because I did really like this girl but I am glad my mum was able to help me see that this was not a healthy relationship and that it is just not healthy to feel entirely responsible for someone else's feelings and for them being OK.

Who is anxious attachment a problem for?

Because we are always pushing and pulling and don't get the things we need from our relationships, anxious attachment is a real problem for creating intense emotions but also for struggling to find healthy ways to manage them. But intense emotions also have a big impact on those close to us and can make them feel as if they have to walk on eggshells, or need to take care of us as if we are the child and they are the adult...when actually they're our boy/girlfriend or best mate! We can start to get mixed up about what our feelings are that we need to manage and what the problems are within an individual relationship. The best way to work that out is to think about whether or not this is a repeating pattern or position that you find yourself in across a number of relationships, if this is where you often end up. If it's the position that you often end up in, and the feelings are familiar and similar across those relationships, then it's more likely that it's something it would be helpful to think about and work on yourself. If this is a new experience, then it's more likely that this is something that is specific to this particular relationship and you need to talk it out with the other person.

What can I do about it?

We're not going to lie to you. It can be difficult to step out of patterns and take risks in relationships when the fear of rejection and being alone can be huge. But it can be done! What we know is that we can't just promise people (or ourselves) or simply wish it was different – it's a process that needs time, effort and ideally a safe person to help you think things through.

Understand your patterns

In Chapter 2, we talked about writing your story or 'formulation'. If you have done this, it will be helpful when you're trying to work out what interactions or relationships are causing you to feel upset, anxious or distressed as you have some ideas about what your 'key fears' are and what you do to try to cope with them. If you've not done this yet, then it might be an idea to nip back to Chapter 2 and have a go. It's not a quick exercise but it will be helpful in moving forward.

If you know what you experience as 'threats' in your relationships (such as being ridiculed or being abandoned) or what your personal core pain/key fears are about your feelings and internal experiences (e.g. that you will get overwhelmed with intense emotions and lose control), then being able to find ways out of the patterns in your relationships becomes much easier. It's important that you are kind to yourself as self-criticism and negative self-talk will only make you feel worse and turn to others for reassurance. It's more likely to make you feel that others 'deserve better' and make it harder to be a healthy adult in your relationships with the right balance between support and independence. The process of formulation used in Chapter 2 promotes and encourages a compassionate approach to yourself, your story and your relationships.

Once you have an understanding of your story you can move forward with the next steps.

Notice

The first thing you need to do is *stop* and be aware of when you start to experience intense emotions in your relationships. What are your 'hot spots' or triggers for when you start to feel intense emotions, feel overwhelmed or feel a frantic urge to keep the person close at all costs and your thoughts start to predict bad things? Notice if the same things are causing problems in a few relationships or are themes in painful or difficult interactions. You need to be able to recognize the patterns you fall into before you can do anything helpful to try to change them.

Recognize and revise

You need to spot patterns then use all of the strategies in the chapter to try to find new ways to respond.

Take a pause

The beliefs we hold about ourselves and others are not easy to bring to mind especially when emotions are intense. When you get overwhelmed by feelings and think that they were 'caused' by someone else, you may respond quickly and can be 'reactive' (we call this being in 'emotional mind' – see Chapter 10). You might feel embarrassed about these reactions afterwards and feel as if they're hard to control. It can be super helpful just to take a few deep breaths or actually say, 'I just need to take a ten-minute time out. I don't want to just react' to stop yourself using only the feelings and falling into saying and doing the same unhelpful things. Taking the pause can soothe the body and calm your mind, so you stop your early experiences or fears driving how you respond to others rather than the actual person or situation in front of you (see Chapter 10 about using your wise mind).

Own your feelings

One of the most important things is to be clear that your feelings are your own and you're responsible for them. This doesn't mean you're able to control them all the time or can change them, but that they're yours.

It's common that because you might see the feeling as simply a reaction to a betrayal/thoughtlessness/rejection then you might blame the other person, *'You made me feel this way! This is your fault!'* Although your feelings have been triggered by whatever they have done, often when you have intense feelings this is because they're reminding you of *old* hurts and rejections. The person in front of you may well be confused by your intense emotions. Of course, some betrayals, losses or rejections are just extremely painful and would hurt no matter what your previous experiences were. But what we find with young people who are really struggling is that it's often everyday stuff that is triggering big feelings. Little things like someone saying 'no' (to the cinema maybe) or ignoring us (when they were just busy doing Sudoku) are constantly reminding us of old wounds and maintaining core beliefs that 'I am invisible/not important' and 'Others will leave or reject me'.

A good simple starting point is to change your language from 'You made me feel' to 'When you did/said that I felt...' so you're reminding them and you that their behaviour is part of the picture but not all of it. Feelings are complicated.

Find ways to soothe yourself and feel OK in your body

Once you are aware of what is setting off the intense emotions, it's important that you find the things that help you to soothe and regulate those feelings in your body. This is the focus of this book and so we hope you can find the things that work for you right here in these pages!

Once you have found the things that make you feel good, you can think more clearly and are able to do one of the most difficult bits...

Let others know what you need from them

One of the common myths about 'good' relationships is that people just 'get it' and you don't have to tell them what you are thinking, feeling, and how to make you feel OK. This is quite simply complete rubbish. Relationships which work well are usually when both people communicate clearly about what they think, feel and need from the other person and can also let them know when they have crossed a line or 'boundary' without being hostile or punishing them. Being able to say 'no' and 'that is not OK' are really important but can be tough when you are terrified of the other person rejecting you. This is another thing you will need to be aware of, work on and practise to get better at it. This means asserting yourself and not letting things build up so that you end up rejecting them or being angry and aggressive. Practising out loud saying, 'I didn't like it when you...' and finding a way of wording things that feels comfortable can be helpful. Or if your friend/partner knows that you're trying to make a change then maybe write them a letter that tells them what you really appreciate about them and what you find difficult (e.g. 'Sometimes I overreact when you need some time alone because I feel worried that you're going to reject me'). This takes a lot of trust. See Chapter 12 for more strategies for being able to say 'no' or assert your views in relationships.

Keep a journal

It can be helpful to keep a journal to help you reflect on your intense emotions and how they're impacting on your relationships, and how your relationships affect your emotions. Recording in a journal allows you to think about stuff when you feel calmer. Getting your feelings out on the page can be helpful in taking the heat out of your feelings, but most importantly it makes it easier to spot thoughts, themes or patterns that keep coming up. Also, thinking when you're calm means you get a different, hopefully clearer, perspective on your emotions or what ways of coping you might fall back on when you feel overwhelmed. It will also help you record and see when you're managing to step aside from unhelpful patterns and realize the impact of doing things differently.

Write letters (that you never send)

We know that being able to talk to important people who may have affected the way that you feel and how you cope with intense emotions can be difficult or even impossible. It might be that they're not around anymore, or that they're not someone safe who can listen and tune in. Writing letters that you don't send is a safe way to access feelings that maybe feel too difficult to talk about and to be mindful about taking a compassionate stance of recognizing that others were nearly always just coping in the best way they knew how. Sue has also done this in therapy with people, where rather than writing a letter, they choose a chair in the room and pretend that the person that they want to talk to is sitting in it. They then have the opportunity to talk to this person in a safe way, airing all of their feelings, fears and wishes, without any potential comeback. This chair in Sue's office has been ex-boyfriends, dads who have left the family home, critical bosses and many other people (it's very good at acting). Although this might sound like an unusual thing to do, you might find that once you start writing (or talking), lots of thoughts or feelings come tumbling out. This can then help you to express and process (get through) these big feelings in a safe way. When doing any of these exercises, it can help to have a safe person with you who can help or support you after the exercise.

Get the balance right

Another important thing can be to practise doing things on your own and developing your skills at coping alone. We are not suggesting that you need to stop spending time with your family, friends or boy-/girlfriend, but that you try to make sure that you're spending some time alone and developing your confidence. When you start to practise 'riding the waves' of intense emotions, you will be able to see that you're able to cope with lots of these feelings without support, as they simply pass with time and some deep breaths. You might just delay making the call and take a few mindful breaths or repeat a mantra, 'I am strong, this feeling is rough, but I am plenty good enough', so you feel more in control before you share your feelings and seek some support to show yourself that you can do it on your own. There's no shame at all in needing support, but it's also important to get the balance right and build your confidence and skills at riding the waves alone sometimes, so the panic doesn't set in if there's not someone there with you.

Be a scientist observer

An active way to try to avoid simply reacting is to purposefully take a 'scientist observer' position and try out some new things.

Once you notice your triggers (girlfriend doesn't call back) and the associated thoughts of, 'She is going to leave me', then you are likely to have an urge to call her or send another message (or ten). So, you might do a bit of an experiment, 'I predict she won't get in touch', but then you have to fight the urge to react in your usual way...'I will not call or message. I will use my self-soothe and distraction techniques to stay calm and wait until tomorrow to get in touch and see what the outcome is.'

If you're used to people getting frustrated or rejecting you because you're a bit full on, it can be interesting to see that actually if you can resist the urge, manage the emotions a different way, then things might go a lot more smoothly in your relationships.

Another example (a tough one) might be if you feel that if you don't go to every night out then you will lose your friends and they will move on. So, testing this out by sitting home with Netflix and popcorn and the dog might be really tough as you are fighting all the anxious thoughts and feelings about being rejected and losing important people. However, there are two powerful outcomes of this experiment. You managed all those awful thoughts and feelings (using strategies from this book, of course) *and* you didn't really lose any friends. You might have felt left out when they were talking about something hilarious that happened, but it's actually totally manageable. Trying things out in this way may seem scary but it can have really powerful lessons for us. Be brave.

≥ Chapter 5 ≤

Bottle, Bottle, Bang!

So, when you start to think about how to cope with big feelings, you first need to be able to recognize that you are having big feelings. This might sound even more obvious than the breathing malarkey (see Chapter 6), but trust us, this is important. Nearly as important as breathing! When you are busy and stressed out, you often just go from one thing to another, simply reacting to your environment. 'I bit Mum's head off because she said the wrong thing again', 'I fell out with a friend because they were trying to put me down', 'I felt anxious in that class because the teacher is mean.' All those things could be true. Parents (well most people) have an ability to say the wrong thing when they are feeling overwhelmed.

The problem is, we tend to look outside ourselves for the reasons for our behaviour, when a lot of the time the answer is on the inside. Sound cryptic? We don't mean to be, but emotions can be tricky.

Is this chapter for me?

If you read (or abandoned) the last chapter thinking that you couldn't imagine being so bothered about other people liking you and being close to you, and felt weirded out by the idea of *needing* other people to feel OK, then you may have developed a slightly different way to manage your relationships and emotions. It's a way that is really valued in many cultures, which is essentially to pretend that you only have positive or neutral feelings. That you're just fine thank you very much, and you don't need any help or support with emotions from anyone else because you can deal with difficult stuff by yourself – you convince yourself it isn't even that difficult anyway. It is a relatively common term in the English-speaking world to talk about 'bottling things up'. This means that you don't share or talk about what you're thinking and feeling. You might hear phrases commonly used such as 'man up' or 'be strong' – both of these seem to suggest that you should just be able to get on with things and ignore any difficulties that you might be experiencing. But as mental health professionals, we know that this isn't a healthy way of coping in the long-term.

Why do I bottle things up?

Often being self-reliant and suppressing feelings is another really clever way that we adapt to our environment when we're little. As a child, if we find that adults struggle with our emotions and it makes them overreact (such as getting angry, upset or worried) or reject/ ignore us, then we just learn to get on with it and ignore any feelings that might make problems. This can feel safer. This way of coping also makes you a popular child in some ways because you're making zero demands so it's self-reinforcing; but it also means you don't get your needs met and don't ever learn that other people can 'get it' and tolerate your emotions when you need them to.

Sometimes this way of managing feelings and relationships ('I am OK; I don't need anything; I can cope alone') is very hard to change because you learned when you were very young that adults just were not around for you and couldn't take care of you or your emotions. Some people who experienced neglect when they were little genuinely disconnect from the feelings in their bodies. When you are little, if no one comes when you need changing or cleaning then you become really sore, itchy and uncomfortable. The clever way little children deal with this is to cut off from the feelings in their bodies. It really helps at the time, but then as they get older, it can make understanding emotions difficult. Similarly, if you experience a difficult or traumatic time in your life, you can consciously or unconsciously disconnect from the memories or thoughts and pretend it never happened. This is a common strategy for children and adolescents who cannot physically remove themselves from awful situations so learn to 'go off in their head' to avoid the difficult or even unbearable emotions. We call this 'dissociation'.

We know for most people, thankfully, their parents were taking care of them just fine, but we also know that many parents don't respond well to intense emotions. Sometimes adults think it's helpful to ignore intense emotions to make them go away (they may have even read this in an 'expert' parenting book). However, actually, we know that when adults ignore communication and intense emotions in their child, this is usually painful, humiliating and often confusing for the child, so they have more negative stuff going on and no adult to help them feel OK again (that co-regulation we talked about in Chapter 2).

Why might parents struggle with their child's emotions?

It's true that for lots of adults, their child's intense emotions are really hard to deal with and in some countries (namely the UK) it's common for people to think that it is ridiculous and embarrassing to have feelings at all! So how do they manage when their toddler is having a screaming tantrum in a public space or is inconsolable because they lost an old rag they like to carry round? As popular children's author Dr Seuss says, 'A person's a person, no matter how small' and a toddler's grief at losing his rag can be just as important and overwhelming as an adult's grief. All parents get overwhelmed by their child's feelings sometimes. That is normal and understandable, but if this happens regularly and consistently, then their child has got to learn a way to deal with it and feel OK – this usually means learning to ignore and suppress intense emotions, so the child can pretend that they don't exist.

This is not us parent bashing. We know that parents are simply coping with difficult things and their own intense emotions in the best way they know how. Some parents care a *lot* about their child's feelings and want them always to feel OK, so much so that any distress the child shows makes them feel anxious and out of control so they do everything they can to make them feel better and protect them (wanting to wrap them in cotton wool). The problem is that this can feel overwhelming and intrusive to the child, so they *also* learn to shut down and suppress feelings to avoid this overwhelming response from their parent or carer. In this case, ignoring the feelings works well because then they don't have to deal with all the parent's anxiety and reactions.

Can someone else have helped me with my emotions instead?

If you become self-sufficient at recognizing and managing emotions through the help of another adult, teacher, older brother or sister, or later in life through a partner or best friend, then you're winning. These new relationships can teach you that it is fine to depend on another person and let them see all the feelings, not just the positive or neutral ones, so you can find ways to manage these emotions not just ignore or suppress them. The problems happen when something important occurs in your life that creates intense emotions and suddenly you need to reach out to others and you don't know how. Alternatively, the feelings that you have been able to ignore and suppress get too big and intense to handle, simply because they have been building up over time.

Ways of avoiding emotions

Often, you can find other ways to avoid emotions like being constantly busy, drinking alcohol, eating lots of food or taking excessive exercise. These are very effective ways to avoid difficult thoughts, putting off experiencing intense emotions or simply numbing them (drugs and alcohol) or 'stuffing them down' in the case of over-eating. These strategies can work really well for a long time. You might have become the life and soul of the party or even a successful athlete so these coping strategies can also be very rewarding. The problem is that the intense emotions and the need to connect with other people don't go away so when you hit a crisis you aren't able to reach out and you don't know how to cope alone. Basically, while you are still ignoring how you feel you are not meeting your underlying needs and at some point, you might go 'bang!'

The thing with this (very clever) way of coping with early life is that even if we are amazing at coping alone and not feeling our emotions, it's an undeniable fact that human beings still have intense emotions and a biological need to connect to others. So although you may reach adulthood genuinely feeling that you don't need anyone, a sudden outburst of intense emotions might be your first clue that some stuff is lurking there beneath the apparently OK surface, and that you actually might need people to help and support you sometimes. You may never know exactly what things were like when you were little, but if you recognize yourself as someone who is (overly) self-reliant, doesn't experience or share feelings, and appears calm and rational but then feelings seem to come bursting out of you in rage, anxiety or sadness, then this chapter is really important for you. I'm guessing that if you're reading this book then things are not completely working out for you, with the bottling things up and not depending on anyone, so we will stop trying to convince you.

Triggers: What makes you go bang?

You may know the saying 'the straw that broke the camel's back'. It basically means that if you add one tiny straw at a time, there will be a point where you add one final seemingly weightless straw and the poor camel falls to the ground. It's the weight of the whole bale of straw that breaks it, but there's one final straw that gets the blame... If you're not allowing yourself to communicate with others about your feelings, and not even allowing yourself to really feel them, then it can be the tiniest thing that leads to the intense emotions coming to the surface and bursting out with a bang; for example, losing the plot with your partner over a movie that you don't want to watch or getting uncontrollably angry because someone is rude to you in a coffee shop. This makes it hard for other people (and even you) to understand your feelings, and can make intense emotions seem scary (to other people) and embarrassing (to you).

How can this chapter help me?

If feelings have just burst into your life (and you're not too happy about it), then you might be someone who has come to the end of the line of bottling things up. Alternatively, you might be someone who has always had unexpected outbursts of emotions throughout your life and this has made you scared, embarrassed or worried about these intense emotions taking you over and being out of control. Either way, we have some quick tips (and of course the rest of this book) to help you think about starting to deal with feelings differently. If you're still feeling convinced that ignoring difficult feelings is the way to go, it could be useful (before you abandon the book and go and eat some snacks) to do a quick 'pros and cons' list of what ignoring and suppressing might be costing you, the downsides, as well as the things you think are good about it. This can also help motivate you when you notice that you are falling back into trying to ignore and suppress feelings. Or maybe this strategy is really working for you and you don't need us at the moment at all. It's important to make changes when you are feeling sure you *want* things to be different, or it's not going to be helpful.

Pros – why ignoring feelings is great	Cons – why ignoring feelings is not so great
1. I don't have the time to deal with them 2. I don't want to look foolish if I start letting feelings out 3. My feelings are not for other people to see. I like that they are private	1. Other people think I am fine when I'm not and this can be upsetting 2. Feelings sometimes burst out and make me feel embarrassed anyway 3. I have got into trouble at college/work for my outbursts 4. My girlfriend thinks I don't really like her when actually I do

Example of pros and cons list

When we work with young people, we often talk with them about 'avoidant attachment' and describe the bottle of fizzy drink that gets shaken up until the lid flies off and the drink goes everywhere in a dramatic plume of froth. How can this literal (and emotional) mess be avoided? Well, as any fizzy drink lover knows, you have to do tiny little turns on the cap, letting out teeny weeny squirts of fizz until you can calmly do your last turn and enjoy your (slightly flat) drink. This book is basically about finding the ways to turn your regulation 'cap' and let emotions out in healthy ways so that they feel manageable and there is much less mess.

Reconnecting with your body

When you have spent years ignoring what's going on in your body, it's important to take the time to start to consciously think about where sensations and emotions are carried or felt in your body. Start with easier feelings before you try to tackle some of the more difficult and distressing ones. When I'm calm, where do I feel the sensation of being at rest? When I'm happy, can I locate the contentment in my face, stomach, arms, legs? Taking short pauses throughout the day to check-in with yourself and what's going on in your body is helpful and important. If you can gently reconnect and be aware of sensations in your body and where your emotions make themselves known, you'll be much more likely to be able to get in there early and try some of the techniques we talk about later in the book when emotions are building up.

Spot your 'warning signs'

It might feel as if you just 'blow,' but we bet you that there are subtle warning signs that intense emotions are on their way out. They might be internal ones that you need to be able to spot in your body, like getting hotter, or they might be things that you aren't aware of that other people can see...like your facial expression or eye contact. It can help to get someone who knows you well to help you make a list of what happens before you 'blow' and write them down on a card that you carry round (or on your phone), with some helpful ways to stop the feelings building up anymore (there are lots of examples of this throughout the book). It can be hard to think straight once the intense emotions are starting to make themselves known so having stuff written down (in your plan in Chapter 14) can be really helpful.

Reconnecting with others

The problem with pretending everything is fine most of the time and bottling things up is that other people like this cool attitude – until the BANG and then they really don't. It might be that you don't ever let the people you love see the BANG so they are still clueless, but we would guess that there's still a problem connecting with others when you're hiding intense emotions or not allowing yourself to feel them because these feelings are an important part of *you*. Some people can be great at reading even what you are hiding, but this is *hard work* and often others will get tired of it and start to feel as if you don't care or are not really 'in it'.

We know that letting others know about your emotions can sound really scary, but a bit like the stuff about becoming aware of positive feelings in your body, you can take it slowly and start off with some of the easier emotions and things that feel safer, and start to test out what might happen – just as in the previous chapter where we asked you to test out your predictions about what might happen if you were terrified of being rejected. It can also be really helpful to let other people know in advance how they can help you when you are feeling low/worried/angry. It might be that you just want them to check-in on you if they notice you going quiet, or to make you a hot drink, or sit with you watching TV. One way of doing this can be to share your self-care plan with those close to you (see Chapter 14), so that they can understand you a bit better and what kind of things might help.

EMMA'S STORY

Since being a child, I've been a bit avoidant of emotions. I quickly learned, growing up, that it was safer not to show my feelings to anyone, but to keep them in and try to ignore them. Being the eldest of my siblings, I perhaps had to grow up more quickly and I tried to protect my younger sisters from what was going on at home. My mum was quite a scary woman – to me anyway. To the outside world, she wanted us to appear to be the perfect family and she physically looked after me (fed me, made sure that I had clothes and a nice bedroom). But she would often lose it, scream and shout at me when no one was looking that she hated me, she wished I had never been born, that I was worth nothing. It was as if she blamed me for everything. She found every excuse to accuse me of things, even if I had done nothing wrong. She would follow me round the house screaming at me, and I would lock myself in the bathroom while she screamed on the other side of the door.

Although my dad was physically present in the home, he was drunk most evenings (I think that he drank in order to cope with my mum), so he wasn't much use to me or my siblings. But the worst thing was that I believed what my mum was saying – that I was worthless, unloved and not as good as other people. I never told anyone. I didn't think that other people would really care, that they would laugh or make fun of me if I told them what was going on or how I was feeling, or that they would just ignore me. I thought that it was just my 'job' to get on with things and try to ignore what was happening at home. From the outside, I probably looked as if things were going OK. I was doing well at school and I had friends. But underneath I felt absolutely shit. As I got older, I started to plan my 'escape route' from home, and this was my way of coping – whenever things got really bad, I would just think about how I could get away in a few years' time.

What I didn't realize at the time was that my feelings were bubbling under the surface. When I was in my teens, I started to have panic attacks. At first, I didn't know what these were, but just knew that I suddenly felt overwhelmed, couldn't breathe, felt dizzy and needed to 'get the hell out of there'. Now looking back, I know that this was my body's way of telling me that something was wrong. Then I discovered alcohol. This became one of my coping strategies – I could block out how I was feeling and forget for a while what was happening at home. But I started getting so drunk that my friends were becoming annoyed with me and stopped wanting to hang out, and the morning after drinking, I felt even worse. Of course, my mum didn't like this either, so this made things even worse at home.

As I started to develop closer friendships and had my first girlfriends, the idea of depending on someone else or trusting them with my innermost thoughts and feelings was incredibly scary. What if they saw the 'real me' and started to hate me too? I found myself initially pushing them away. When something was on my mind, I would never tell anyone but would try to sort it out by myself. But then sometimes, when things were really bad, I felt as if I was drowning.

It has felt like a really big journey for me, but after some brief therapy, and starting to learn more about myself and my 'patterns', I have slowly (very slowly) started to let people in. I now know that if I'm feeling rubbish or struggling with something, it's important to let someone close to me know, even if it's just so that I've shared it with someone. They don't even need to do something to help, but just listen or give me a hug. Sometimes it can feel really hard to do this, and I get stuck with my thoughts of 'I should do this myself, they won't want to know, or they've got their own stuff going on.' But over time, I'm starting to challenge myself over this and let people in more. Sometimes I get to the stage where I'm emotionally full, and I need to take some time to look after myself and let other people know how they can help me out. People around me also know to check-in with me if they think that I'm getting stressed, and this really helps, so that I don't have to start the conversation with them first.

Part 2

WHAT CAN HELP – INTENSE EMOTIONS

In Part 2, we explore coping strategies that can help you to cope with intense emotions. Chapter 6 focuses on getting the basics right, such as your sleep, diet and exercise, as we know that these can help us to feel OK in our bodies. We then start to think about ways to soothe difficult or painful feelings, suggesting coping strategies which will help you to transform or feel more in control of your emotions and learn to cope in a crisis. When reading through Part 2, you might want to keep a note of strategies that you find helpful, then you can put them together into a self-care plan at the end of the book.

≳ Chapter 6 ≲

Getting the Basics Right

Feeling OK in Your Body

This chapter is about the things we need to do to feel OK in our bodies because essentially emotions are feelings that are not just experienced in our minds, but as physical sensations in our body. Emotions are complicated and can sometimes feel too intense to handle. Before we start thinking about the different ways that you can cope with feelings, we always talk to the young people we work with about 'getting the basics right' and taking care of what their body needs to feel OK.

There are a few reasons why feelings might get too overwhelming. One is that you're just one of those sensitive people who feels things more intensely than other people. Your body has a bigger reaction to the things going on around you, which can be great when you're feeling lots of positive things like excitement and joy, but can be difficult when there's stressful, messy or horrible things happening around you. We know that some people, from when they were babies, have bigger stress reactions in their bodies when new things happen, whether these are good or bad. The other reason that people experience feelings more intensely is because they're just being faced with too many stressful situations and they don't have another person to help them feel OK (see Chapter 2). The final reason might be that you try not to feel your emotions, you block them out and ignore them. The thing with feelings is, they're just part of being human. When you ignore them, they sort of bubble and bubble away until BANG, they come bursting out. We will talk more about these ideas later in the book. First, we think that no matter what the reason is for your overwhelming feelings – whether it's being sensitive, facing big problems as a young person or bottling feelings up – getting the basics right will make you feel better in your body and give you the starting point for being able to feel awesome and in control.

Breathing

OK, so we know that you don't need to read a book to know how to breathe. If Sue and Bridie had a quid for every hard stare or eye roll they'd had from a stressed-out young person dealing with intense feelings when they talked about breathing, they could buy every reader a cake for their birthday.

The reason we talk about it so much is because it's *really* important. Breathing is key to regulating (calming) our body's stress response and overwhelming feelings. You know how people always say, 'Take a deep breath'? Well, they say it so much because it's actually a great way of managing stress and feeling more in control of the feelings in our bodies. The problem is that often people just say, 'Take a deep breath' and when you have an overwhelming feeling this can feel like a fob off and you need to know a little bit more. It can also be really hard to focus on your breathing when you are panicking or feeling really distressed as there is so much going on in your head. When you breathe in, you activate your body's sympathetic nervous system, your heart rate starts to go up, blood flow increases to certain parts of your body and muscle tension increases. But when you breathe out, you activate the opposite system, 'parasympathetic', which encourages blood flow to your stomach and digestive system, slows down your heart rate and reduces tension in your muscles. So, when you want to slow things down a bit, you need to breathe out longer than you breathe in to help the body calm and soothe itself. The problem is that when you feel overwhelmed you can often do short shallow breaths, and the way your brain and body respond can make you feel as if you can't breathe so you need to take bigger breaths in to get more air and counteract the feelings of tension/tightness in your chest. But this is a mean old trick! What you really need to do is take a deep breath in, but then take an even longer breath out.

Bridie tells her young children to take 'dragon breaths', where they pretend to be a dragon breathing fire slowly out of their nostrils. This might sound as if it's meant for tiny people, but it's a good way to remember what you need to do when you want to be strong and in control. We also talk about 7–11 breathing, which simply means counting to 7 while you breathe in and extending your out-breath to the count of 11. Doing this for just two minutes (you can use your watch to time it) can really help to make you feel better in your body. It can be helpful to watch your body and check that you're breathing from your stomach and that your stomach is rising and filling up with air as you breathe in, then slowly going down as you breathe out. This way you know you're not doing the shallow breathing that can contribute to feeling out of control. Here are some other breathing exercises:

Soothing rhythm breathing: Sit or lie down comfortably. Close your eyes if you can or choose a spot in the room on which to gently focus your gaze. Place one or both of your hands on your stomach (if using both hands, you can interlock your fingers). Breathe in slowly and notice your stomach and hand rise with your breath. Then slowly breathe out, again noticing your hand lowering as your stomach lowers. Notice the pace of your breathing, and the rise and fall of your stomach and gently slow it down, allowing it to be slower and deeper, until it feels comforting and soothing. Everyone has a slightly different breathing pattern that feels soothing to them, so play about with yours a little until you find one that helps you to feel relaxed and comfortable.

Bubble breathing: If you feel comfortable, close your eyes, or gently rest your focus on a space in the room. Put one hand on your chest, and one on your stomach. Feel your chest rise on the in-breath and fall on the out-breath. Take slow breaths. Breathe in through your nose, then hold your breath for a count of five. Then breathe out through your mouth slowly, as if you were blowing a big bubble. Make sure that your out-breaths are longer than your in-breaths.

Blow bubbles: Alternatively, using a wand and bubble solution, slowly blow some bubbles. You might want to control your breathing and slow down to blow big bubbles – see how big you can make them. You might want to blow lots of tiny bubbles. You then might want to catch some of the bubbles on your wand. It can be worth trying out lots of different types of bubble solution to find the ones that work best for you.

We don't advise constantly thinking about your breathing (as you need to be getting on with other stuff!), but just being aware of your breaths and making sure you're sat or standing in an open posture and allowing your breath to enter and leave your body smoothly, knowing that you need to breathe long and slowly when you're under stress is a good start for feeling calm and in control.

Getting a good night's sleep

Sleep is so important for helping you to manage big feelings. If you struggle to sleep, this can make you feel much more moody or irritable, or slow down your thinking. This can then make you less able to problem solve and use your 'pause' button to help you think about feelings and how best to manage them. We also know that when people are struggling with difficult things going on in their lives or feeling as if they cannot manage their feelings, this can stop them from sleeping properly. So, you get stuck in a vicious cycle.

Why is sleep important?

Although sleep might seem like a time when your body is relaxed and slowed down, or even switched off, this is definitely not the case. During sleep, your body is highly active, doing things that are important for your body and mind to function properly. Lots of physical things happen when you sleep, including your muscles recovering from all their use during the day and some important hormones (like growth hormone) being produced; sleep even helps you to grow! Importantly, it also helps you to process your emotions from the day, so a lack of sleep can lead to struggling with feelings. You might also notice yourself feeling more on edge, anxious or giddy. It seems as if the brain knows that you are lacking in energy, so it gives you a rush of feelings so that you can keep going. As discussed in Chapter 3 about your brain, young people also need more sleep than adults to function.

Sleep also helps you to use your mind effectively – without it, you can struggle to concentrate during the day, you might forget things, or feel disoriented or even confused, making it hard to think clearly. Research has suggested that sleep is essential for our brains to naturally reset, which helps us to remember things and learn. Without a good night's sleep, you can therefore struggle physically, emotionally and mentally.

What is the right amount of sleep?

The amount of sleep needed for a healthy life changes as you grow older. Also, everyone is a bit different. Some people might be typically longer sleepers and some shorter sleepers. However, the average sleep 'requirements' are as follows:

- Age 5–13 years – approximately nine to eleven hours per night

- Age 13–18 years – approximately eight to ten hours per night

- Age 18 and older – approximately seven to nine hours per night, but this gets a bit less in later life.

Your sleeping patterns

First, let's think a bit more about your sleep and where you might get stuck. If you understand more about your own sleeping patterns, such as the quality as well as quantity of your sleep, it can help you to think about what might improve it. It might also be useful to show your answers to someone close to you, to see if they can identify where you might be struggling.

Most nights...

- What time do you start your bedtime routine (e.g. putting PJs on, brushing teeth)?

- What do you do between your bedtime routine and sleep (e.g. check phone, watch TV)?

- What time do you usually go to bed?

- How long is it generally before you go to sleep?

- How many times do you wake up in the night?

- How long are you usually awake for?

- How much sleep, in total, do you get on an average night?

- How many nights of the week do you struggle with your sleep?

- How would you describe your sleep?

- Do you feel refreshed after a night's sleep or still tired?

During the day...

- Do you still feel tired?

- Do you struggle to concentrate?

- Do you feel moody?

- What impact do your sleeping patterns have on your life?

- What would be better if you could sleep more?

- What have you already tried to get a better night's sleep?

- What makes it more difficult to sleep?

Five ways to get a good night's sleep

This section gives you six different ways to improve your sleep, including thinking about how to improve your bedtime routine, the environment that you sleep in, helping your body and mind to relax, avoiding things that are likely to keep you awake, and minimizing distractions. Perhaps try some of these out and see which ones work for you. You can monitor their impact if you wish, using the sleep chart at the end of this chapter.

1 Make your bedroom a sleep sanctuary

The place that you're sleeping in can have a massive impact on your ability to get to sleep and your quality of sleep. Some people can sleep pretty much anywhere, such as on a noisy train. But other people will struggle much more and might need a place where they can relax their body into a comfortable position, with limited distractions around them and stimulation (we mostly mean noise or light).

To help you feel comfortable, try to get the temperature right so that you're not too hot or cold. A cooler room with enough blankets to stay warm is generally best. A room that is too hot or one that is too cold can mean you feel restless and wake up more often. Opening the window for a little while before going to sleep can help to get the air in the room moving and make the room feel less stuffy.

Make the room dark and quiet. Some people like to just make their room completely silent (e.g. closing the door, removing noisy items) or even wear ear plugs to block out noises that might disturb their sleep. Other people like listening to relaxing music or sounds as they're drifting off to sleep. Too much light in the room can make it difficult to fall asleep. You could use a sleep mask or black-out blinds to keep the light out.

2 Get a good routine

One of the best ways of training your body to sleep well is to get into a routine and to go to bed and get up at more or less the same time every day. This gets your body used to the pattern, so it's ready for sleep when you go to bed. Although it can be really tempting to take a nap during the day, particularly if you have not slept much the night before, it's best not to unless it's less than 20 minutes in the morning. If you take long naps later in the day, this can further disrupt your sleeping patterns at night, making you less sleepy or tired, or not wanting to go to bed. Even if you had a bad night's sleep and are feeling super tired, try your best to keep your daytime activities the same as you had planned.

It's also better to only try to sleep when you actually feel tired or sleepy, rather than spending too much time awake in bed. If you haven't been able to get to sleep after about 20 minutes, get up and do something calming or boring until you feel sleepy, then get back into bed and try again (but if you can't fall asleep after about 20 minutes, then get up again...and keep going).

You can find your own sleep rituals to try to remind your body that it's time to sleep – some people find it helps to do relaxation stretches or breathing exercises or have a cup of non-caffeinated tea before going to bed.

3 Things to avoid

When we want to relax our body and mind, we need to slow down our thinking and calm the feelings in our bodies. Some of the things that we eat, drink and breathe will be unhelpful and make us feel more awake, alert and even hyperactive. These include caffeine, cigarettes and alcohol. So, it's best to avoid these for at least four hours (if not more) before going to bed. Energy drinks should also be totally avoided, as although they may make you feel less tired at the time, they're going to stop you from being able to get to sleep later. If you dance or do exercise in the evenings, it's best to do this as early as possible so that you have time to relax your mind and body before going to bed. Some people really enjoy having a small supper before going to bed (mmm toast!) and this can actually be helpful for sleep. However, it's usually best not to have a big meal later on – small snacks are better.

4 Minimizing distractions

In order to relax your mind, it helps to attempt to shut off from everyday distractions and demands. You can train your mind to get ready for sleep by following a good sleep routine (see point 2), but sometimes this can be difficult if you are distracted by other things which can take up your focus and attention. Wherever possible, try not to use your bed for anything other than sleeping, so that your body starts to associate your bed with sleep. If you use your bed as a place to watch TV, eat or work on your laptop, then your body will not learn the bed-sleep connection.

One of the biggest things that stops most people (including us) from sleeping is looking at our phones. It can be so tempting to just check something on the internet or see why it beeped, but this will bring your mind straight out of your sleep routine and back into being active. Even worse than this, recent research has told us that time looking at screens (such as your phone) can cause sleep problems, such as poorer quality sleep and taking longer to fall asleep. There is a biological reason for this, as there is a blue light which shines out of your phone (and other devices) and prevents a sleep hormone called melatonin being released. The level of this hormone usually increases a few hours before you go to sleep and is like a signal to the body to prepare you for sleep. So, when this hormone is not released, it will be far more difficult for you to fall asleep. Also, the lights behind the screens of devices can cause the brain to be more alert (tricking the brain into thinking that it's daytime), getting in the way of a good night's sleep even more! Although lots of you may end up going on your phones and looking through your social media accounts, this is likely to delay and interrupt your sleep routines. It will keep your minds busy and active and you might get drawn into a conversation or worry. We often say to young people and their families to have an agreement where you plug the phone in downstairs at 8pm for the night so that it cannot get in the way of a good night's sleep.

Another big distraction that people often talk about is watching the time. When you're struggling to sleep, it can be easy to keep checking the time to see how long it has been since you last checked and how long it is until the morning. However, checking the time during the night is likely to reinforce unhelpful thoughts such as , 'It's so late, I can't sleep' or, 'I've only slept for four hours'. These thoughts can make you feel anxious or frustrated, and even less likely to fall asleep. It can also have an even worse effect if you check the time on your phone (see above information about the screens of devices). So, try to check the time less and only when you really need to.

Eating well

As well as getting a good night's sleep it's important to make sure that you're eating a balanced diet with lots of fresh fruit and vegetables.

This might seem like another eye rolling nag to have at someone when they're feeling overwhelmed by emotions, but when we are stressed out this can mean we forget about healthy eating, eat more junk and sugar to try to soothe our feelings, or because we feel yuck we stop eating at regular meal times. This is a problem because it creates and affects all sorts of feelings and sensations in our bodies. If we are not eating regularly, or not eating the right foods, then sudden surges and drops in our blood sugar can mean we do not feel OK in our body at all. We can lack energy or feel a bit giddy or cycle between the two. Trying to make sure that you're eating healthy food at mealtimes, with regular nutritious snacks, is a good starting point for feeling OK and able to cope when life throws us some stress and triggers big feelings.

Exercise

There's now a lot of research and a growing understanding that being active is vital to psychological wellbeing and feeling better in our bodies.

When we say exercise, we don't mean going to the gym (Sue is good at this...Bridie is not). Activity that improves your mood and mental health can range from walking more steps each day, to running marathons. Things that might take your fancy include dance classes, rock climbing, horse riding, playing a sport or swimming in a cold lake!

So how does it help? Well, exercise releases lots of chemicals in the brain that we know are associated with feeling good in our bodies and a sense of wellbeing. These chemicals are things that we know get out of balance when people feel low in mood, anxious, are struggling with concentration or attention, or when they have faced traumatic experiences. Exercise gets the good chemicals going. Exercise is known to improve sleep (see section above) and to improve energy levels throughout the day. Physical activity and the way it makes you feel can then be a coping strategy that you use instead of harmful things like eating junk food or drinking alcohol that actually make you feel worse in the long run. As well as the chemicals, there is often a sense of mastery and achievement (I ran further/faster, or climbed higher, learned a difficult dance routine) and this boosts mood and resilience further.

The problem is getting active in a realistic way that will keep going rather than burn out. Bridie is great at charging out of the house with her trainers on determined to run 5k and do that three times a week until she is a shining beacon of physical and mental health, but she runs too fast and gets too far from the house, thinks she might die, then has to walk home red and breathless with sore calves and swears to never run again...till the next time she feels rubbish and needs to get active. Making big changes and big commitments is never a good idea. Slowly increasing the amount you walk and signing up to an activity that you want to try with a friend once a week is a good place to start. For example, there are apps like *Couch to 5K*, which helps you to start running from scratch. Sue uses some mindfulness running apps including Headspace's *Not Motivated Run* and *Running on Empty*.

Drugs and alcohol

So when we feel overwhelmed by intense emotions and we don't feel OK in our body, one way that people find makes them feel calm again is to drink alcohol or to use substances that change the way that they feel both physically and emotionally. They may use a substance to stop their mind racing and their body feeling tense or they may use something else that makes them feel 'buzzed' and confident to talk to others if they usually feel heavy and slow and worry about how others see them.

Although adolescence is a time of experimentation and risk taking, it feels important to say that substances can be helpful in making us feel better in the short term, but sadly the long-term impact of this can make our intense emotions worse and prevent us finding healthy and helpful ways to deal with feelings. We don't develop the positive routines and activities that can sustain feeling calm and OK more of the time and for a longer time. Chapter 13 has some ideas for sources of support if you're worried about using substances to cope with intense emotions.

Chapter 7

Self-Soothing

This chapter explores the concept of self-soothing. It helps you to think about how you can use your body, and your senses, to feel OK again, calmer and back in control. Your body can often get into states when you are either over-aroused or under-aroused. Sometimes you might feel slowed down and exhausted, and you cannot even consider doing what you are supposed to. It might feel way too hard to even contemplate getting out of bed, and you might want to hide under the covers and never come out. At other times, you might feel full of emotion and overwhelmed, so incredibly emotional (e.g. angry, distressed, giddy, panicked) that you cannot focus on what you're meant to be doing, but just feel carried away with the emotion. This chapter therefore helps you to think about how you can enable your body and mind to return to a state of calmness and feel OK again. It goes through a menu of different self-soothing exercises, so that you can try them out and see what works best for you.

Deep pressure and resistance exercises

The following exercises and activities can help your body to feel grounded and calm.

Leg massage: Sit down and put one of your hands around each ankle (allow your head to fall below your knees if this feels comfortable). Apply firm pressure and then rub upwards along your legs, slowly. Repeat a few times until you feel calmer.

Drinking through a straw: When you drink through a straw, this creates some resistance, as your body (mouth) has to work harder to get the drink, which in turn can help you to feel calmer and more focused. So perhaps get a straw for your water bottle.

Hand massage: This can be a nice exercise to either do yourself or to ask someone close to you to do. Imagine that you're putting the difficult feelings under your thumb. Place your palm upwards and use your other thumb to massage the palm of your hand up to ten times. Then repeat with the other palm and thumb. You might want to then rub along all of your fingers right up to the tips. Sue tends to do this with scented hand cream.

Sitting on a gym ball: This can be a good strategy to use whether you're feeling overwhelmed, distressed or exhausted. It can also be quite tricky and uses up a lot of concentration. Find a gym or yoga ball and put it in a place that is safe and where you're unlikely to hurt yourself if you fall off it. You can sit on the ball with both of your feet planted firmly on the ground. Try to sit still and relax. Alternatively, lie on your stomach on the ball with your flat palms on the floor at the sides of the ball and your feet reaching all the way to the floor.

Progressive muscle relaxation: Lie on your back, as flat as possible, with your arms at your sides. Tense your facial muscles, screwing up your face, for a count of six. Then, as you breathe out, let go of any tension and relax. Tense the muscles in your shoulders, bringing them up to your ears, for a count of six. As you breathe out, let go of any tension and relax. Repeat this with your arm muscles and hands; your back muscles (bringing your shoulder blades downwards); your stomach; your bottom; the tops of your legs, your thighs and knees; your lower legs, calves and ankles; and your feet, curling your toes upwards. Then, as you breathe out, relax.

Swivel chairs: In Sue's office, her team of psychologists all have swivel chairs, and you may see them spinning around the office regularly rather than getting up and walking (partly because they're lazy, partly because they like the sensory 'input' that it gives to them).

Rocking chair: Alternatively, you might like the sensation of sitting on a rocking chair, if you have access to one, and then rocking in a slow, controlled manner.

Covering your eyes: Rub the palms of your hands together briefly to warm them. Then, take a deep breath and place your palms gently over your eyes. Continue to breathe in and out, taking deep, slow breaths, and feeling the warmth from your palms over your eyes.

Foot squeeze: If you have someone to do this for you, having a foot squeeze or massage can be a nice way of getting some deep pressure, which can help you to feel grounded and calmer.

Push the wall: With your feet flat on the floor, stand up facing the wall, with your palms flat on the wall, and push as hard as you can for ten seconds (although make sure that the wall is sturdy enough first!). Alternatively, it might feel soothing to sit next to a wall. For example, sitting on your bed and leaning your back onto the wall (perhaps with a cushion between you and the wall).

Den with pillows: Making a space where you can cram in lots of pillows/cushions and blankets, which then give your body a nice big squeeze can help you to feel calm and regulated. Similarly, asking someone that you're close to, like a parent/carer or partner, to place pillows on your back/legs and then put some firm pressure (but not too hard) on them, may also feel soothing.

Weighted blanket: Also, using a weighted blanket (a blanket with weights sewn into it) or a few heavy blankets can feel soothing, as if you're having a big hug. These can be particularly useful when you're feeling really distressed or overwhelmed.

Wearing a backpack: If you wear a backpack that is quite heavy (but not so heavy that it hurts your back!) this can also be helpful to make you feel calmer.

Yoga exercises

There are also several exercises that you can do with your whole body that can help you to feel more in control of yourself physically and emotionally. These can be useful to do first thing in the morning, last thing at night (before bed), or at any time in the day when you have a yoga (or other suitable) mat with you. We won't describe them in this book as we aren't yoga experts, but would suggest that you look at exercises such as Downward Facing Dog; Upward Facing Dog, Bow Pose, Reverse Table, Child's Pose, Sunrise/Sunset and Windmill. These are all described well in Lauren Brukner's 2017 book, *Stay Cool and In Control with the Keep-Calm Guru*, or there are lots of videos online.

Sensory soothing

Sounds

Some people like listening to soothing sounds such as the sound of a waterfall, a babbling brook, the waves in the sea crashing, birds tweeting, rustling leaves, rainforest sounds or the sound of rain. You might also like listening to relaxing music or songs. Some people like listening to beautiful or soothing music; others might prefer exciting or happy music (maybe make a playlist of your favourite tracks). Alternatively, you might want to use audio recordings of guided mindfulness or relaxation exercises. Think about which music you listen to and match it to your mood. For example, if you're feeling exhausted and unmotivated, make sure that you choose a track that helps you to feel energized (such as one with a quick tempo). If you're feeling distressed or overwhelmed, perhaps choose a more calming track.

Touch

You may like to touch things that are silky and smooth, or soft and comfortable (such as fleece), or even things with a rough or abrasive texture. You might have a scarf, hat or gloves that feel soothing to the touch that you can wear or take out of the house with you. Some people enjoy snuggling under a blanket or heavy duvet (or making a duvet fort). Having a hug from someone you care about can be quite soothing or you may just want to hold their hand. You might also choose to hug a cuddly toy or pillow. Put on a large dressing gown or clothes that you can relax in (such as big, baggy clothes). Perhaps hide under your duvet for a bit or wrap yourself up in a warm, comfy blanket. Some people enjoy the sensation of putting body lotion on their skin, which can be even more sensory if it has a nice smell, or using a foot soak.

Alternatively, body scrubs can give a stronger sensation on the skin and may feel tingly afterwards (although don't scrub too hard!). It may be useful to find out whether you feel more soothed when feeling warm or cold – everyone is different. If you like the warmth, then wrapping up, a warm bath or shower, fluffy socks or a hot water bottle might be pleasurable. But, if you prefer the cold, you may enjoy a cold flannel on your face, running your hands under cold water or a cold glass of water or a drink with ice in it. Using cold items can sometimes help to counteract the warmth you may feel when anxious, from your racing heart and tensed muscles. Sometimes, being able to get rid of some tension in your body through using items can help. For example, lots of people use playdough or putty that they can squash, roll into balls or throw as a way of reducing tension. There are also stress balls, or other foam balls, punch bags, or even punching a pillow.

Smells

What is your favourite smell? Does it help you to feel calm or relaxed? Smells trigger different feelings in people, so it can be useful to work out which ones help you to feel soothed. Some common soothing smells are freshly cut grass, peppermint, lavender and talcum powder. Some people might like the smell of baking or old books. You might have a favourite scent or perfume that you wear, or a scented candle or air freshener for your room. You may also choose to use scented body lotion, bubble bath or shower gel. There are ways of taking soothing smells with you wherever you go, including wearing a scent, spraying the scent on something that you carry with you or having some in a little container.

Sight

Which things do you feel are soothing to look at? You might feel soothed by watching a candle, spending time outside in a field or near to water (e.g. beach) and watching the waves crash onto the shore. You may enjoy watching the clouds float past in the sky. You might feel soothed looking at flowers or plants, so find ways to have these around you if you do. You might like things that remind you of positive, soothing memories such as photographs of family, friends, pets, your favourite sports team or musician, or times when you have felt content, such as on holiday. There might be objects that mean something to you, such a particular piece of jewellery or watch, a certificate that you have won, a leaver's book or card that someone has written, or a special present that someone gave to you. Lots of people have special quotes, positive sayings, mantras or song lyrics that they like – you might want to write these out or print them, and carry them with you (or keep them on your phone). You might have a favourite DVD or book that makes you feel soothed or brighter in mood.

Tastes and textures

When thinking about food and drink, both the taste and texture can be soothing. People's tastes can vary greatly, so again it's about exploring what makes you personally feel soothed. Crunchy foods tend to be good to help people to emotionally regulate, such as pretzels, apples, crisps or chunks of iceberg lettuce that have been in the fridge. You might find cold items nice and cooling (see Chapter 9 for TIPP skills) such as ice lollies, drinks with ice in or grapes that have been in the fridge. You might enjoy the tastes of food such as chocolate, fruit or hot toast, or the comfort of having a warm drink such as tea or coffee. Choose your favourite hot drink and have it in a big mug (if you like hot chocolate, you could even add marshmallows). You may prefer the sensations of foods such as popping candy or sour sweets, which can help to focus your attention on something other than your thoughts (it's really hard to focus on anything else when there are mini-explosions or a sharp sourness in your mouth). There might be foods that remind you of soothing times, such as chicken soup (for times that you have been looked after), creamy mashed potato or ice-cream. Or foods that make you just feel happy when you're eating them – someone once told Sue that however bad they were feeling, they could not help but smile when they were eating jelly. When you're feeling rubbish, it can often be difficult to find the motivation to go out to the shop to get these things, so it may be helpful to make sure that you have access to some soothing food items in your house. For example, you may choose to keep a sachet of your favourite hot drink or a special treat food (e.g. small bar of chocolate) nearby.

Whatever it is you find soothing, the important thing is to have it available and easy to access at times when you might need it. You might choose to have a fluffy blanket in your room, a supply of special hot chocolate or a playlist of your favourite soothing music on your phone – whatever works for you. Another way that people might make their soothing items easily available is by creating a self-soothe or self-care box (see Chapter 9 for more information).

Relaxing and soothing the mind: Imagery of a safe place

Imagery can be very powerful in helping to calm down our minds. There are lots of types of imagery that we can do, but here is an exercise that you can try out. When doing the exercise below, find somewhere to sit or lie down where you're unlikely to be disturbed. The more you practise when you're feeling calm or things are still, the easier it will be to use when you're starting to struggle. It can be useful to have a trusted person helping you to do these exercises, perhaps reading out the scripts to you or helping you to build on the images that you create. Also, the image might not come to you straightaway, or it might come and go, or change over time. All of these are absolutely fine...sometimes you might get a colour or shape or sound and this might be enough. It's just about bringing to mind whatever is soothing to you.

Safe place

When feeling intense emotions, it can sometimes be nice to go away in your mind to a calmer, more peaceful place. Often people choose to imagine a beach, a field or floating in the sea. However, it's important to find somewhere that feels calming and relaxing to you.

In this imagery exercise, just allow a safe place to gently emerge from your mind and see what appears. Gently close your eyes and relax your body. Allow your breathing to slow down to a comfortable pace, with any tension flowing out of your body on each out-breath. When you feel ready, take a few steps forward in your mind, walking slowly into your safe place. Imagine a space that feels safe and soothing to you. It could be something from a memory, or something completely made up. Just allow feelings of safeness and calmness to flow around you. Imagine yourself feeling calm, relaxed, safe and soothed in this space.

Look around you – what does your safe place look like? What kind of colours, shapes, textures are there? What smells do you notice? Freshly cut grass? Baking? The saltiness of the sea? What can you feel? The hard ground underneath you? The sand beneath your toes? The sun on your face? You might be drawn to a field with long grass with the sun beating down on your face and a bright blue sky. Or you might be in a den full of cushions and duvets. Or perhaps lying back floating in the sea. Or outside in a beautiful winter wonderland. Or snuggled up in front of a roaring fire, with a fluffy dog sitting on your feet and the smell of cookies baking in the oven. Allow these sights to come and go naturally in your mind but stay with the feeling of safeness and calmness. When you feel ready, allow yourself to slowly walk out of your safe place and back into the room. You might want to wiggle your toes to slowly bring you back.

Now that you have started to discover what your safe place might look like, it can help to practise this and build on it. You might want to think about the questions above and start to write a description down of what can help you feel safe and soothed, or you might want to draw pictures or find photographs from the internet.

All soothed out

With this chapter, it can be useful to try out the different strategies and practise them when you're feeling calmer, rather than just when you're feeling overwhelmed. There's an analogy about a swimming pool that always comes to mind – you wouldn't (I hope!) learn to swim by jumping straight into the deep end without armbands because you're likely to drown. You would start at the shallow end with your inflatables and practise swimming first, and slowly build up your confidence before tackling the deeper waters. It's a similar thing with the coping strategies that we discuss in this book. Rather than attempting them for the first time when you're having a full-blown meltdown, perhaps try them out when you're feeling calm or just a little bit stressed, and then work your way up, using them as needed.

> Chapter 8 <

Riding Your Emotions

Do you ever feel as if you just can't get rid of a difficult feeling (like sadness, frustration or anxiety)? As if it won't go away and you're stuck in it forever?

Sometimes the way that we react to our emotions can unintentionally prolong them. So, when we're trying to get rid of our emotions by pushing them away or trying to forget about them (see Chapter 5), or alternatively focusing on our thoughts or bodily reactions, it can actually make them worse. Also, sometimes we can start to judge ourselves for having the emotion in the first place, which can add another (often even more) unpleasant emotion to the initial one. For example, if we are feeling sad, we might start to judge ourselves for feeling like that (I shouldn't be feeling that way), which can make us annoyed at ourselves. Then we are left feeling both annoyed and sad! Or if we're feeling worried about something, we can sometimes start to feel worried about our worrying, which can lead to double worrying! So, it's important to consider how we think about, and react to, our emotions.

When you feel intense emotional pain, it can be all-consuming, so much so that you can't see a life without the painful emotion.

This is not just you being dramatic. When you're in the middle of overwhelming feelings, thoughts and chemicals bouncing around everywhere, it can be very difficult to see a way out. However, what we know is that the emotional response will eventually end, as all emotions do. Over time, they start to run out of fuel. Often emotions will gently rise and fall, like waves in the sea. We talk about finding ways to 'ride the waves' of your emotions – learning that you can *sit with* the emotion and survive it.

HAPPY SAD JOYFUL GLOOMY COSY GRATEFUL NICE EXCITED SELF CONCIOUS ANGRY LOVING

Naming and taming our emotions

One of the main ways of calming our emotions is to label them. Psychiatrist Daniel Siegel calls this 'name it to tame it', as research has found that when we're able to name our feelings, we're more able to control them, and they have less of an impact on us. When we tell ourselves (or others) 'I feel worried', this allows us to understand worry as a feeling rather than something that we are (i.e. I am worried). When we label our feelings, it therefore helps us to understand them better and then work towards finding solutions or helping ourselves to feel better. So being able to recognize and name your emotions can be a really good first step.

THE 12 CORE EMOTIONS

JOY Sadness ANGER Fear

SURPRISE L♡VE DISGUST
Guilt

Interest
Jealousy

SHAME ENVY

Although many of the above emotions might sound familiar, people often get stuck on the differences between guilt and shame. When we talk about guilt, we mean feeling bad about your actions (what you've done); whereas shame is feeling distressed or humiliated about yourself (feeling that you're bad or shameful). Both are painful emotions, but shame tends to make us feel really rubbish, and it can feel impossible to shift, whereas guilt usually motivates us to make a repair with the person we have hurt or to think about making different choices next time.

As well as recognizing and labelling our emotions, we can take this to another level and start to investigate them using mindfulness. This means that we can learn to notice, allow and accept the feelings that we have in our bodies – 'riding the waves'. Step back and observe the feelings as you experience them in your body. Where can you feel them (in your arms, face, heart area, legs)? What are the sensations like? How intense are the sensations? What shape are they? Do they come and go or stay the same? Stay curious and investigate what you're experiencing. Then it can be useful to take a few deep breaths and allow the sensations to 'just be'. Don't fight against them or struggle with them, just allow them and wait for them to pass. Sometimes you might be fearful that they won't pass, but they always do. Remind yourself that these are normal bodily reactions and make peace with them. This mindfulness of feelings can be difficult, particularly at first, and especially if you are having a lot of intense, difficult feelings. But when you've managed to ride the wave of feelings once or twice, and have watched them eventually stop, it can build up your confidence to be able to ride the wave again.

Acting the opposite

As we know, our feelings and behaviours are often interlinked. You feel a particular way, and then you get an urge to act in an associated way too. For example, if you wake up feeling low or sad, you might have the urge to stay in bed all day under the covers. This is called an 'action urge'.

EMOTIONS AND THEIR ACTION URGES

Joy – to seek out more of it

Sadness – to withdraw

Fear – to fight, flight or freeze

Anger – to attack

Love – to attach/keep close

Envy – to take

Jealousy – to guard

Guilt – to repair

Shame – to hide

Disgust – to repel

Interest – to get closer

Surprise – to pause and assess

It's important to understand that there's a big difference between having an urge and acting on it. We will all have some intense emotions that can create strong urges to do a number of actions such as hitting people, screaming, hurting ourselves and throwing things. Having the urge isn't a problem, but it can become a problem if we choose to act on it. So, it can be useful to recognize when we're having an action urge, but then be able to pause for a moment to decide what to do. Sometimes it can feel that our urges are so powerful that we *have* to act on them, but this isn't the case. But, sometimes, it can take a bit of practice to learn to pause and break this link between the urge and action.

Try it out yourself for a moment. Sit on your hands (both of them). Then when you're ready, imagine that you have a tickle on the end of your nose. Feel it really starting to tickle. Then notice your urge to want to scratch it, but don't. Feel the urge, but don't act on it. Even if it feels really uncomfortable, just notice that you're having the urge but don't act on it...

OK, you can now scratch your nose!

There's a technique in dialectical behaviour therapy which is called 'opposite action'. In a nutshell, this means doing the opposite to what the emotion is making you want to do. So you need to recognize any urges, pause and then identify an alternative, more helpful, way of responding. This skill is great to use when your emotion is unjustified (such as if you feel shame but haven't done anything wrong), and it can help you to reduce that unwanted emotion. You can also use it if you are feeling stuck in a particular emotion. However, it isn't useful if the emotion you have is needed. For example, if your house is on fire, you don't want to sit calmly and do some mindfulness.

When thinking about the opposite action technique, it's useful to think about how the emotion might look and feel, so that you can fully embrace the opposite. We're talking facial expression, body language, thoughts, tone of voice, what you say and what you do. For example, you might feel fearful about meeting a friend in town for a coffee, and as you start to walk into town you have the urge to turn away and run home (flight). So, after a few deep breaths, you might decide to take the opposite action and walk into town, appearing confident, thinking, 'I can do this, this will be enjoyable', with relaxed body language (letting go of any tension), talking confidently and facing your fear. Or, if you were feeling angry towards your boss because they were asking you to stay late at work, you might have the urge to shout at them or send an angry email (attack). But, if you were doing the opposite action, you would take a few deep breaths, relax your shoulders and posture, and, using a calm voice, would speak to them and assert your views or raise your concerns.

USING OPPOSITE ACTION

Pause

1. What emotion are you feeling right now?

2. What action urge are you feeling that fits with the emotion?

3. Will acting on the urge be helpful for you?

4. Do you want to change how you are feeling?

5. If yes, what would be the opposite action?

6. Do the opposite action – make sure that you do it all the ways that you can (facial expressions, body language, tone of voice, thoughts, words, behaviour).

7. Keep doing the opposite action until the emotion reduces.

Distraction

Another helpful strategy to help you to ride the waves is distraction, which can temporarily take your mind off the difficult feelings and help to divert your focus onto something more enjoyable. This can then help you to tolerate your difficult emotions when they feel unmanageable. The best distractions are ones that grab your attention and leave you feeling absorbed in the activity.

What kind of things do you do, or have you done, that take up all of your attention or make you focus and concentrate on the task (not leaving much space to think of other things)? Examples might include: playing a game (board game/computer game), doing intense exercise or playing sport, listening to loud music and singing along, doing a really hard puzzle, trying to sing your favourite song backwards (this is hard!) or counting backwards from 100 in fours. You might enjoy doing crafty activities (such as sewing, drawing), reading a book, baking or playing on a computer game. Sue has found that when she feels rubbish then goes to a spinning class, where she has to really, really focus to keep herself going (as all she can feel is the aching in her legs), then this activity fully absorbs her. The sad feelings completely go away. Afterwards, she is left feeling exhausted (from all the physical activity), but also much, much calmer and happier.

Alternatively, you might want to do something that's likely to bring up another emotion for you. For example, if you're feeling sad, you might want to do something that usually makes you feel happy, such as watching funny videos or listening to a comedy podcast or fast/bouncy music (if you like that kind of thing). If you're feeling angry, you might want to listen to calming music or snuggle up in a blanket. If you're feeling worried, you might want to sing aloud loudly to your favourite songs.

Another activity that you can do which may improve your mood is what we call 'contributing' – this is when you do something to help someone else, thus bringing your attention to their needs rather than your own. This could be making a hot drink for a family member, helping your sister with her homework, doing some chores around the house, writing a message to a loved one to say something nice or check-in with them, looking through your cupboards for things to take to the charity shop, or cooking a meal for a friend. These small acts of kindness might make someone else smile, and then make you feel a little lighter or happier too.

Cope ahead plan

Now that you've hopefully found some strategies that might help you to be able to ride the waves of your emotions more easily (from Chapters 6, 7 and this one), it can be useful to start to think about how you can put these in place, especially in situations that you know are going to be difficult for you. One way to do this is to create a cope ahead plan (CAP). This is a detailed plan for a situation you know might trigger painful emotions, setting out how you're going to cope with it. The idea is that at the time that you're going through the situation it's likely to be hard to think about what to do, and what will help you to feel better in the moment. This can then lead you to act in an impulsive way, based on how you are feeling at the time (emotional mind), which you might later regret. So, if you have a plan in place already, you'll know what to do and you can use the strategies that help. It can also make you feel more confident about going into the situation in the first place.

There are four main steps to making a CAP:

1. Describe the situation that you think might cause intense emotions for you.

2. Think about anything that you can put in place that can help you beforehand, such as making sure that you get enough sleep the night before, having a good breakfast, putting your clothes out ready the night before so you have less to think about in the morning, going for a run.

3. Decide what coping strategies are likely to help you at the time, such as getting a cold, fizzy drink, taking a few deep breaths (bubble breathing), planning to spend time with a friend afterwards watching your favourite films (see p.98).

4. Imagine the situation and think through how you will use the skills. You can even role-play if you wish to.

EXAMPLE OF A COPE AHEAD PLAN

Situation: I've got a meeting with my boss at work. I know that I'm not meeting my targets, so it's likely to be a meeting about this. He really talks down to me and it winds me up. Last time we ended in having a big argument in the middle of the office and I nearly got sacked.

Preparation: Go to bed early the night before. Talk to a friend who I know can help me to think through things clearly, about what I want to say and how I can say it.

Coping strategies: Check-in with my body/how I'm feeling and do some muscle relaxation (especially for tension in my shoulders). Listen to my favourite podcast on my way into work. If I feel overwhelmed, drink some water with ice, or go to the bathroom and splash my face with water. Have a bubble bath when I get home.

⋟ Chapter 9 ⋞

Coping in a Crisis

In this chapter, we'll explore different techniques that can help you in a crisis. We simply mean an event that causes you a great deal of distress and feels absolutely overwhelming. When you're experiencing painful emotions such as distress, you can act in impulsive ways such as shouting or screaming at people, drinking alcohol or throwing things. The problem with these coping strategies is that although they might give you some temporary relief (it might feel great to throw something across the room), there's often a consequence (when you realize that it was your phone). In the last few chapters, we have talked about more general coping strategies to improve your mood and help you to cope with the ebb and flow of intense emotions, but it's not always easy to use these when you're feeling at your most distressed and overwhelmed. So the techniques in this chapter focus on when you feel that the wave is about to take you over and crash down on you. We aim to help you to ride the wave (and learn that you can survive it) until you feel calm enough to use some of the other strategies. These techniques are often called 'distress tolerance' which means learning to cope with, and ride the wave of, your difficult feelings (rather than ignoring them or trying to get rid of them). Luckily, this chapter is going to give you a guide to tolerating those overwhelming emotions and will give you some essential tools to add to your tool kit.

The thinking line

First, we want to introduce something called the thinking line. Most of the time we all sit somewhere below the line, which means that we're able to think clearly. We can make rational decisions, see the bigger picture, we're aware of the benefits and consequences and we can generally cope with our emotions. However, if something happens that causes us distress, our wave goes above that thinking line and our ability to think clearly reduces. This means that we struggle to think, make sense of what is happening and potentially lose touch with reality, which can lead us to act on impulse and make unhelpful decisions, possibly putting ourselves or others at risk. This impulsive way of coping with our emotions can lead to self-destructive behaviours or aggression towards others (see Chapter 8). The good thing is that you can't stay above the thinking line forever. It may be for 15 minutes, an hour or three hours, but you always come back below the thinking line and start to feel calmer again, and your thinking brain re-engages. But later you can feel confusion or regret about what happened.

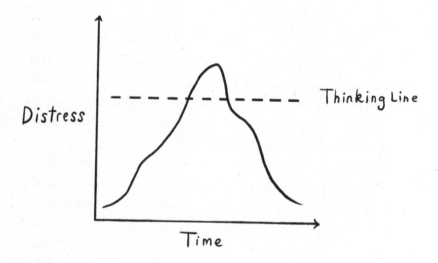

Imagine a time when you've felt really distressed or in a crisis. Can you remember what was happening in your body and mind?

When you're above the thinking line, this is usually when your body goes into 'survival mode'. This is your 'fight, flight, freeze' response which is the clever way that humans have evolved to respond in a crisis. The threat brain is the oldest part of the brain, right at the base of your skull, and it sets off your fight, flight, freeze response using stress hormones. When the threat brain is activated, it bypasses or shuts down the most developed and social bit of your brain, the frontal cortex, just behind your forehead. Your frontal cortex is responsible for empathy, problem solving and language, so in a 'threat' situation (when you're feeling distressed and above the thinking line) it makes sense that you simply shut this bit down. It wouldn't be very helpful to go through the pros and cons of each possible action if you are being stalked by a sabre-toothed tiger – you're basically dead by the time you have tried to work out if he looks hungry. Your three simple choices are to fight off the predator, run as fast as you can (flight) or play dead (freeze). So, this is why, when you're feeling distressed, you're above the thinking line and so are less able to think clearly, focus or concentrate and see the wider picture. This basically means that you can easily make regrettable (or plain stupid) decisions when you're in a crisis, as you can't think through things as you usually would. Can you think of any times when you've felt so distressed that you couldn't think clearly? When you're in survival mode, your body also starts to get ready for action, preparing you for fight or flight. This means that your heart starts to beat faster, your muscles tense, your breathing quickens and you might find yourself getting hot and sweaty. This is preparing you to cope with whatever happens next. It can be helpful if you're in physical danger, and can potentially keep you safe. But the response isn't necessarily helpful when you are psychologically fearful, for example being scared of being rejected or humiliated. The last thing you want is sweaty hands when you're about to meet someone new, or to go into an exam with shaking hands so you can't write.

TIPP skills

As outlined above, when you are feeling distressed and overwhelmed, you're unlikely to be thinking clearly and are more likely to act in an impulsive way. So, TIPP skills aim to calm your bodily reactions, in the short term, and bring you back below the thinking line, so that you can get some space to think. This then stops you from being so impulsive and doing things that you will later regret. You then can go back and deal with the situation in a calmer, more thought-out way later. They also can help you to feel much better in the moment and calm that wave before it crashes. TIPP skills aim to rapidly reduce the intensity of your emotions by 'tipping your body chemistry'. They activate the parasympathetic nervous system which helps you to slow down your bodily responses. They are easier than some of the other skills to use when you're in a crisis, as they don't take much thinking, and they can be really effective (as long as you're doing them properly). But, as we said before, they aim to provide a short-term relief to your distress, giving you space to feel calmer and think about how to react to the situation.

TIPP

Temperature
Intense exercise
Paced breathing
Progressive muscle relaxation

The technique TIPP is a distress tolerance skill which works by changing your body chemistry. There are four ways you can do this: by lowering your body temperature; intensely exercising; using paced breathing and practising progressive muscle relation (we will explain what these are as we go along). Sometimes you may only need to use one of the techniques, but depending on how distressed you're feeling, you might have to use more. When you start, these techniques might feel overwhelming or strange, but the more you use them the easier they become. Remember, it takes 21 days of practising to form a habit!

Tipping the temperature

(This technique should *not* be used by people with certain medical problems such as heart disorders, anorexia and bulimia. If you have any concerns, please speak to a medical professional before using this skill.)

When you're angry or upset, do you find yourself with fiery red cheeks and feeling very sweaty? If so, using ice cold water to cool yourself down will help lower your core body temperature. By doing this, you can reduce your heart rate and start the process of coming back below the thinking line. When we put a cold compress onto our face, it activates something called the 'dive reflex' which leads to our heart rate suddenly reducing to below resting levels. There are many ways that you can tip the temperature of your face, such as splashing your face with cold water (or putting your face briefly into the sink), holding a cold compress on your face, or holding a cold can to your face (lovely, when straight out of the fridge). If you're somewhere public, you could go to the bathroom and splash your face with water until you can feel your heart rate starting to slow down. You can also run your hands under cold water and splash your face, or perhaps have a cold drink or ice lolly. You can also put ice in a ziplock bag and keep it in your freezer, and then when you need it, you can hold the bag against your face, just below your eyes. One way to enhance the effects of this technique is to hold your breath for 10–20 seconds while doing it. Hannah's favourite way to use this skill at home is to hop into a really cold shower, even with her clothes on if she needs to calm down quickly. She can find it useful to stay in for at least five minutes, to have time to regulate her breathing and ensure that her body temperature stays down.

LOUISE'S STORY

I started to use the Tipping temperature skill at first at home, when I would get frustrated with my partner or my cats (when they were litter training but not quite there yet), and would open the fridge to feel cool air on my face. Then, when I started work in a fast-food restaurant, I did the same thing in the big fridge when I was dealing with difficult customers. It made me relax and feel much calmer before I went out and dealt with the situation.

Intense exercise

Intense exercise isn't always the most attractive option for some of us, but if it works, it works. When your body is in survival mode and ready to fight or flight, it's really hard not to act impulsively. So, when we do intense exercise, it can help us to get rid of any tension, or excess energy, and help us to feel regulated again. You can do any exercise you like as long as it's intense and gets your legs aching and heart racing. Some good ones to try are a few minutes of jumping jacks or two to five minutes of sprinting (and we mean sprinting) on the spot, or put your favourite music on and dance non-stop. Even exercising for 30 seconds might help, as long as it's super intense! This way you can put all your energy into exercising, and it can help your body to start to calm down and your mind start to think more clearly.

Paced breathing

Your breathing can become out of sync in a crisis, and it's likely to have speeded up, which can create even more distress. The best way to combat this is to focus on slowing down your breathing and making sure that your out-breath is longer than your in-breath. This then activates your parasympathetic nervous system and calms down your emotional response. It might help to count as you breathe, for example, breathing in for a count of four, then breathing out for a count of six. This is a simple and discreet skill that you can use anywhere. If you struggle to count for yourself, you might want to use a breathing exercise app. There are examples of more breathing exercises in Chapter 6 – try them out and see which ones work for you.

Progressive muscle relaxation

This last of the four skills is a bit longer and is easiest to carry out when lying or sitting down (but with practice you'll be able to do this anywhere). This relaxation exercise focuses on tensing and relaxing each muscle group in your body, which leads them to return to a more relaxed state. It can help you to relieve tension in your muscles, slow down your body and calm your emotions. There are many ways you can access this exercise. If you have access to the internet you can find lots of videos that will talk you through the relaxation, or see Chapter 7 for a step-by-step guide on how to carry it out.

Useful tips when practising TIPP

- Don't forget that practice makes perfect. You may find it useful to write the acronym out and stick it around your room and take a picture of it so that if you're above the thinking line and can't remember what to do, you'll have it right in front of you.

- Sometimes one skill might not work, but remember to try the other ones too. It may be helpful to make a TIPP diary and every time you use one (or two) of the techniques, note down your distress as a score out of ten before and after the exercise. That way you can work out which ones work well for you.

- TIPP isn't going to make everything better, but it will bring you back below the thinking line again so you can have space to think.

STOP technique

Another useful tool to add to your crisis survival kit is a technique called STOP.

Stop
Take a step back
Observe
Proceed mindfully

Sometimes it's difficult to notice when you're in a crisis or to identify that you're edging towards some really painful, overwhelming emotions. When you have overwhelming emotions and become 'above the thinking line', you can make impulsive decisions that will probably not be helpful in the long term or could end up being something you regret. So, the Stop technique literally gets you to stop and evaluate how you're feeling and how best to manage those feelings.

Imagine people shouting horrible names at you while going down the corridor in college. You feel so many emotions: embarrassed, sad, maybe even frightened. And then all of a sudden, you get an overwhelming feeling to go and face-push the person shouting at you (please don't do this, violence never solves anything!). However, the good thing is you that know the skill STOP and you're going to use it to your greatest advantage.

1. First, when you get the burning desire or thought to push the mean person over you will notice it, *Stop* and stand still.

2. Then you will *take a step back* and look at the situation as if you're watching the scene on closed-circuit TV. Give yourself

some time to breathe and calm down. You could carry out some paced breathing to give yourself some time, so you don't feel the need to act immediately. Focus on your breathing for as long as you need to.

3. After this, you need to *observe* the situation and work out the facts so you can make an effective decision. How did you get into the situation? What are the pros and cons to acting on your anger? How will it affect you in the long term?

4. Then you will *proceed mindfully*, asking yourself what want you want to gain from this situation and what the best way to proceed is that will benefit your goals.

If you were the person in the situation above, you might feel overwhelmed by the desire to face-push the person, and in the short term that might give you a sense of satisfaction. However, if you did push them, you might later (when you're back below the thinking line and feeling OK again) regret what you did and might even feel worse than you were feeling at the time. It's always good to give yourself some time out before making decisions when in a crisis, especially if these decisions could hurt you or someone else. By giving yourself some time out, you have a period of time to bring your mind and emotions below the thinking line so you know you can make an informed decision that sits with your personal values. You'll need to practise this skill and it might not go right every time. A good way to practise is to make up a scenario – if you want to have some fun with it, you could make it a bit silly, or you could choose a situation that you think that you're likely to experience. Once you've thought of a situation, write down how you would cope with it using the steps above. You could also do this with other people and compare your responses at the end. Don't forget your journey to managing overwhelming feelings is a marathon, not a sprint.

Crisis box

When you experience overwhelming emotions, it's always a good idea to have some things/skills on stand-by to help you to ride the wave – be prepared! Making a box with things that you know will help you when you can't think straight is ideal. You don't have to call it a crisis box – you could call it your calming box, happy box, self-soothing box or [insert your own name]'s box. It's unique and personal to you, so there's no right or wrong way to do it.

You will need:

- Shoebox or decorative box.

- Paints/paper/glue/craft paper to decorate box (whatever you fancy).

- Sensory items that you find soothing (see Chapter 7).

- Some of your favourite, comforting things.

Other things that could be helpful:

- A list of skills that you know help you when you're in a crisis.

- A list of people you can call, with their numbers (including helplines as well as family/friends).

- A letter to yourself (that you've written previously) cheering you on and reminding you of your goals.

- Photos of important people in your life.

- Distractions such as a pen and paper to doodle on, or a puzzle book.

- Positive quotes.

Simply decorate the box as you wish (perhaps design it yourself so that it's particularly appealing to you) and use it to collect and store things that you can use to get you through a crisis. Put the box somewhere that you can easily find it, so you can open it up and use the things inside it when you're feeling overwhelming emotions. If you are someone who self-harms and you want to try to use this as another way of coping, then maybe put the box where you would usually put the items that you use to self-harm, so when you're experiencing those intense emotions, you can access the box instead. You might want to include photographs or nice memories. You can include anything that is going to help you to feel soothed.

LOUISE'S SELF-CARE BOX

I use my box all the time. I've tried to make it part of my routine to just take five for myself and be mindful for the day I've had. It is so difficult making time for yourself! So you should book an appointment with relaxing. I keep candles, a small teddy bear for cuddles, bubbles, pictures of people who make me happy, positive word clouds, bubble wrap and other fidget things, nice toiletries (bath bombs, hand lotions, smellies), reading and colouring books, posh pens, paper, sticky notes and envelopes to write down stuff, and an MP3 player. I also use it when I'm struggling with emotions or in a crisis. Having a self-care box reminds me to take the time to look after myself. It is easy to get lost in the chaos of today's society and having my box in sight just nudges me to take five. Also, when I'm in crisis and needing a quick or simple coping strategy, I don't have to stress out trying to think about what to do. I just go to my box, sit on the floor and open it, and just try things until I find something that works.

When you're stuck in a whirlwind of painful emotions it can feel as if it's never going to end. But, it will...eventually. If you use the strategies above and don't give the emotion any more fuel (see Chapter 8), then it will end even sooner. A quote from writer and motivational speaker Vivian Greene that resonates with us is, 'Life isn't about waiting for the storm to pass, it's about learning to dance in the rain.' Using crisis coping strategies is dancing in the rain.

Chapter 10

Being a Wise Owl

Do you ever find yourself doing things that you know that you shouldn't really be doing? Or thinking that you're doing the right thing at the time but then regretting it later?

Sometimes we can get so caught up in our emotions and how we feel about a situation, that we can't think clearly about what to do – even if, or sometimes *particularly* if, someone is telling us what we should or shouldn't do.

Or you might find that you're someone who tends to make strong logical decisions, considering all the facts about a situation and choosing the option that makes the most logical sense. However, later you might find that you feel really rubbish about the decision that you've made and regret it.

As we found out in Chapter 3 (Understanding Your Brain), as your brain is developing rapidly through your adolescence to become a super brain, sometimes the decisions that you make might be skewed towards how you're feeling, rather than the facts behind a situation. The bit of your brain which is involved in having time to think through situations is developing more slowly, so it can be useful to take some time out to think through decisions from both a logical and emotional perspective, in order to make the best decision that you can.

Being 'wise'

When we talk about being 'wise' what types of images or words does this conjure up? An owl who sits in a tree and observes the world going by? Someone old and knowledgeable? Or is there someone in particular that you know? Generally, when we talk about being 'wise' we mean someone who has a deep understanding based on their experience of life, wisdom and the ability to make sound judgements.

Three states of mind: emotional, rational and wise

In dialectical behavioural therapy (DBT), we talk about the concept of having three states of mind: your emotional mind, your rational mind and your wise mind.

Your emotional mind is when your emotions are completely in control and they influence your thoughts, feelings and behaviour. When using your emotional mind, you would have no inhibitions at all and wouldn't think about what the end result might be. Each emotion also has an 'action urge' which makes us want to act in a particular way. So, if you were 'in' your emotional mind and you felt sad then you would start sobbing and wailing in the street. If you felt angry then you could immediately get the urge to hit someone. You might feel worried and your thoughts might spiral into 'what if, what if'. If you listened to your emotional mind, and responded to it, you may choose to curl up in a corner and never leave the house. It wouldn't be great to live fully in your emotional mind as there would be lots of extreme highs and extreme lows and it would probably feel pretty out of control. What kind of things do you think could lead you to rely on your emotional mind more? Some common examples are feeling hungry, stressed, feeling unwell, tired, or drinking alcohol. But, it's not just bad stuff because being with close friends and something good happening can sometimes make us feel giddy and then do things that we wouldn't usually do.

Your rational mind is the complete opposite. More like a robot or computer, it looks at the facts, statistics and logic of situations and makes decisions based on these, such as assessing how likely things are and what the risks could be by weighing up the facts and, crucially, without taking into account your emotions. It can be seen as cool, calculated and task focused. We need to get stuff done. So, if you were to listen solely to your rational mind, life could be quite boring and unsatisfying as it would not consider how you felt about a situation. It could also affect your relationships as you're less likely to take account of others' emotions – this is a recipe for trouble.

Your wise mind is basically the best of both worlds. It sits in between your emotional and rational minds and listens to both, then makes a decision based on the information it receives (both the 'facts' and how you *feel* about the situation). Some people talk about it being intuitive, a 'gut instinct'.

Let's imagine...you were planning to stay in tonight to complete some coursework that is due in early tomorrow, but you've been invited out to a party. Your emotional mind might be saying – 'You're so bored! Of course you need to go to the party. It will be so much fun (so much more interesting than doing coursework), all your friends will be there, and you can deal with any fall-out tomorrow.' Going to the party will probably give you a shot of positive feelings and satisfies your need for connection and stimulation.

Your rational mind might tell you – 'You have coursework due in first thing tomorrow which you haven't done yet. If you don't hand it in, you're likely to lose marks and affect your grade. You have no reason to miss the deadline and so there's a danger that you will fail that part of the course. If you do fail that part of the course, you may need to do more work to make up for what you've not done.' It's therefore not worth it to go out, and if you stay in you can get the marks you need for the coursework and will not have to do extra work. Staying in will give you the best outcome.

Your wise mind may find it hard to challenge your emotional mind in this instance as the fear of missing out is pretty strong. However, if you choose to listen to your wise mind it would probably say – 'You really want to go to the party and be with your friends, but you also need to get your coursework done to a good enough standard (that you will be happy with). If you go to the party for a couple of hours, realistically your emotional mind will probably take over and you will find it incredibly hard to leave, so that wouldn't work. Perhaps choose not to go to this party, and get your coursework done instead, but plan a fun night with your friends at the weekend that you can look forward to.' Therefore, you'll have met the need for connecting with people and feeling good, but you can also get the positive outcome for your course.

WISE MIND EXERCISE

Take a piece of paper and divide it into three. Think about a recent experience that you have had which has caused you some emotion (not anything too distressing!), such as a fall-out with a friend.

In the first box, write some notes as follows. If your *emotional mind* was completely in control, what would it have you think? What would it have you feel? What would it have you do? What would it want to happen?

In the second box, write some notes as follows. If your *rational mind* was completely in control, what would it have you think? What would it have you feel? What would it have you do? What would it want to happen?

Now channel your *wise mind*. Take a few deep breaths and imagine yourself at your very wisest, full of knowledge and life experience, and full of compassion for yourself and others. In the final box, write some notes as follows. If your *wise mind* was completely in control, what would it have you think? What would it have you feel? What would it have you do? What would it want to happen?

Now just take a few minutes to reflect on your notes and how your states of mind can influence your decision making.

So, one of the best ways to make decisions is to consider both how you feel, what you need to feel OK in your body but also the facts of the situation and what will affect the longer-term outcomes. It can be important to make time and space to step back, take hold of your mind, and think through which state of mind you might be in and what you hope to achieve in the longer term.

The four steps to this would be:

- Step 1: Calm your mind. It's important to make sure that your emotions are regulated (calm) before making big decisions. When you feel calmer your thoughts are clearer, you are more able to access your wise mind and be balanced in your decision making. To do this, you might want to use some of the self-soothing strategies outlined in Chapter 7, or you might just take a few deep breaths, take yourself away to somewhere calmer, or make yourself a hot drink.

- Step 2: How do you emotionally feel about the situation (*emotional mind*)? This is something that you might instinctively know, or something that you might need time to work out. One of the problems with our emotional mind can be that we are not aware of our feelings. One of the best ways to work out your emotions is to talk to someone you trust. Sometimes it can be useful just to speak to one or two people, so that you don't feel overwhelmed by lots of different opinions. Talking through your options with someone and thinking about how you feel about each potential choice might help you to start to understand what emotions are driving your decision making. Another way could be to write down some of your feelings. You may suddenly get a strong response when doing the exercise in Step 3 as to which option you want to choose or which you don't.

- Step 3: What are the facts of the situation (*rational mind*)? One way to do this is to research different options and look at the pros and cons of each option. You might write a list of facts/evidence for each option, then you can directly compare and contrast them. You also might want to talk to people who know more about each option, to get further information about what each might involve.

- Step 4: Make a balanced decision (*wise mind*). So, if you were to take into account both your emotional mind's response, what you need to feel OK, and your rational mind's response to the situation, what would your wise mind think about it? What would a potentially balanced view be (considering both the facts and your emotions)?

Sometimes there is no clear right or wrong decision, and that's fine. We just need to make a 'best guess' about which option to choose, and if this goes 'wrong' then we can choose another option and start again.

What would my wise mind say?

None of us lives in our wise minds all of the time – sometimes it's nice to experience strong emotions and be truly spontaneous and some decisions are best made focusing entirely on the facts and logic. However, if you're struggling with intense emotions and having a lot of difficulties in your relationships, it might be a good indication that you need to spend more time thinking about how emotions are impacting (or not impacting) on your life and ask yourself 'What would my wise mind say?' more often.

GEOFFREY'S STORY

Recently, I had to make the decision of whether or not to move out of my parents' house. I wasn't sure what to do at first. My girlfriend wanted to move in to somewhere that was our own place, and I liked the idea of a bit more freedom. We already lived together at my parents' house. Also, being closer to university would mean that the commute would be much shorter. I felt as if having our own space would be exciting, but I was also a bit worried about the financial side of things. As a university student, I didn't have the option of a proper job, meaning I would be fully reliant on a student loan. However, increasing my student loan for this would impact on my financial wellbeing in the long run, and I had already managed one year of the commute fairly well. So, it was really down to a debate between a bit more independence and financial stability. However, the independence came with its own stresses, as living alone can be a very scary notion. I started to make the decision by talking to people like my mum, and writing lists of the pros and cons. I also made sure that I took time to think it through rather than rushing. I had the feeling throughout that this was what I probably should do, but I left it a few days to think it through a bit more. In the end, I decided it would be best to stay at my parents' house, and I still believe this to be the best decision I could have made. A few months later my girlfriend and I split up, so it was definitely the best decision for me.

Part 3

WHAT CAN HELP – RELATIONSHIPS

In Part 3, we explore what kind of things can help us in our relationships. We think about how to better understand the minds of other people, how to say no, be assertive, and how to repair relationships. We also think a little about how to recognize if a relationship is becoming unhealthy, or even toxic.

Chapter 11

Understanding the Minds of Others

Humans (like those rabbits in Chapter 4) are really good at picking up on the emotional or internal state of other humans. We can know just from watching a good friend cross the road whether he is either filled with joy or has the weight of the world on his shoulders. We're always reading other people and tuning in to what's going on inside them even though we can't ever really *know*. Even when we directly ask what others think, feel, want and intend we're limited by the use of language, social expectations, our assigned roles and many other things. Our amazing ability to reflect on what's going on in our minds and to see what the 'inside' of other people looks like is not even in our awareness most of the time, but it helps us to connect and calm each other. We know that nothing calms an intense emotion like knowing it has been seen and understood by another person.

The thing is that this ability to really understand our own minds and what is going on in the minds of others is not a fixed skill. It's dynamic and keeps changing depending on our level of stress and what else we have going on. Nothing stops us being able to think about another person's thoughts, feelings and intentions like living with them day and night, so the people we are usually worst at tuning in to are the people we love the most. When you can't tune in to others, then you will struggle to understand misunderstandings (that happen all the time) and to understand what you look like to others. Essentially, there will be more conflict and then repairing relationships will be harder.

Mentalizing

The ability to understand yourself and other people through your mental states (thoughts, intentions, beliefs, emotions) is often called 'mentalizing'. When we're 'mentalizing', we have awareness about our own internal worlds (thoughts, feelings, wishes, intentions) and are also aware that other people have their own minds that are separate and different, but which can help us to connect and understand their behaviour and experience. This can be a really hard task to do, as often we don't have a lot of information to help us make sense of what is going on in the minds of others. It's always based in our imagination. For example, you might find it useful if you were aware of what's going on for someone at the moment, how they usually respond in different situations, and the experiences that they have been through (both recently and in the past). However, you can be really good at reading someone just from subtle cues like how they sit and the tone of their voice, if you are relaxed, open and curious. The problems come when you are none of these things and you are feeling stressed or distressed.

How your thoughts and feelings can impact 'mentalizing'

Another way to understand why we get it wrong when we are trying to understand other people's minds is to think about cognitive errors that happen when we're struggling with intense emotions and/or difficult relationships. We know that we are more likely to jump to conclusions and assume the worst about the intentions of others. When we are *feeling* negative emotions, then we can start to think negatively about others and what they might be thinking and feeling. Often, we treat these thoughts as if they're facts because they just feel 'right' and fit with our emotions. When we don't mentalize, we just feel our emotions, we don't reflect on the experience of others' emotions.

For example, feeling: I *feel* unloved. Thought: 'Kirsten is ignoring me because she hates me' = 100 per cent believable thought. Kirsten hates me. Fact. The truth is that Kirsten might just be having a bad day or might have something on her mind leading her to be distracted. Your overwhelmed brain is not really tuning in to your friend but is instead getting caught up in your own emotional state and is not able to reflect on it. Your own emotional state is also dictating your thinking.

Does this ever happen to you? Have a think about any situations where you might have jumped to conclusions or assumed the worst about what another person might be thinking, or why they might be acting in a particular way.

Below we outline some common 'thinking errors' from cognitive behavioural theory that might get in the way of tuning in to others.

COMMON THINKING ERRORS/ASSUMPTIONS

Catastrophizing: This is when we think about something that worries us and we keep going with 'what if' until we reach a total catastrophe. For example, if a friend doesn't reply to a text immediately, you might think, 'They have fallen out with me/they hate me/they won't want to see me again.' Or, when someone in the street smiles at you, you might think, 'They're laughing at my hair nose/outfit...aahhhhh!'

Jumping to conclusions: This is when we use a small amount of information to make a judgement and we come down on the side of caution. For example, if you see that your girlfriend has messaged another man, you might immediately jump to thinking that they're cheating on you, rather than speaking to them about this and seeing what is really going on.

Taking things personally: When we're doing well, humans usually blame the universe for the bad things that happen and take personal credit for when good things happen. It helps us to stay healthy and happy. However, when we are feeling low, anxious or stressed, we can start to blame ourselves for things that have very little or nothing to do with us. For example, if a friend has to cancel a trip to the cinema, you might think that this is because they don't want to spend time with you or that you embarrass them.

Negative filtering: This happens when we ignore all the good stuff that has happened and focus on the bad things. For example, you might become preoccupied with something you said to your boyfriend earlier that day that you felt he might have taken badly, while ignoring the fact that he did not seem bothered by it and spent the rest of the day with you. The negative filter can mean you make a judgement about the whole day and yourself based on only a small amount of negative information and this focus makes you feel horrible. Your brain is tuning in to the negative to keep you safe, but it really ruins your day.

Overgeneralizing: A lot like the negative filter, this means that we use one event or piece of information about something specific to make a global judgement. For example, 'I didn't get invited to the party on Saturday, so everybody hates me.'

Mind reading: Being a human is all about relating to other humans. We are designed and programmed to want to be known and to know other people. However, this important and pretty wonderful bit of being a human can mean we (wrongly) think that we can read people's minds and because we are thinking negatively, we assume they can too. We can then misinterpret intentions and behaviour in a way that is unhelpful. For example, if a person is looking at you on a bus you might think, 'They're judging me, they think I look weird' when you have absolutely no idea what they're actually thinking. They could be admiring your shoes or coat or they could simply be staring straight through you and worrying about what other people on the bus are thinking of them. This kind of mind reading makes us feel awful and is not grounded in reality. This is not mentalizing, this is 'hypermentalizing'.

Black and white thinking: Just like labelling, categorizing things as either 'brilliant' or 'terrible' is a good way to make quick decisions and reason efficiently when there's lots of information available. It takes time to think about and analyse the complexities of people and situations and we don't always have lots of time. If we rely on this kind of thinking, then we can get into trouble. An example of this might be you thinking, 'She looked at me funny when she entered the room, so she's a nasty person and I should avoid her.' However, it might be that the other person was trying to suss you out, and they might want to get to know you as time goes on. They might actually be quite a nice person who was just a bit anxious at first.

Do you recognize yourself using any of these thinking errors? If yes, it might be useful to make a note of these (or highlight them in this book) so that you can start to notice if you're falling into any of these traps when making sense of your interactions with others. The danger of these assumptions is that they stop us paying attention to the people we care about and being curious about what's going on with them, so they don't feel seen, heard or understood, causing misunderstanding and conflict. It also might lead us to react in a confusing or unhelpful way. In the example with poor Kirsten, if you think that she was ignoring you because she hates you, this might lead you to react in an angry way or start to ignore her and cut her out. Kirsten then might feel confused and upset by your anger or worried about why you are ignoring her. Unless you're able to notice and reflect on your thoughts and feelings, then put these assumptions aside, you might hit some trouble. It's helpful once you're calm to talk it through so you can try to understand each other's experience and feelings a bit better.

What do you think could make it more likely for you to struggle to understand the feelings and intentions of others?

That's right. It's the usual. Intense emotions. Not sleeping properly. Not eating properly. Having lots of stressful things happening all at once (so everything seems negative and tests your patience). Feeling rubbish about yourself. Drinking too much (both being drunk and anxious hangovers interfere with how we read people). Feeling physically unwell. Basically, when these things are happening you're less likely to be open or curious because you're just needing to get through and do what you need to do to take care of yourself. Being open and curious and able to get things wrong are key to being able to really tune in to others and work out what is going on for them. If you're bottling things up, then you're not even tuned in to your own feelings, so this can also make tuning in to others hard. When we have space to think, then other people can be interesting and even fascinating...but adolescence is usually a difficult time for this because of what's going on with your brain (see Chapter 3), so you might need some extra help to be curious, open and reflective about yourself and the minds of others.

It is really helpful to take a pause. You may have noticed that this keeps coming up throughout the chapters. We keep saying it because it really is key to managing emotions and relationships. When you do this, you have time to notice what's going on inside you and outside you, and try to calm the feelings in your body before you simply react to your own emotions. Sue likes to take a deep breath, say that she just 'needs a moment', get a drink (ideally something cold) or step outside for a minute or two. Bridie does some weird exercises/dance in the toilet that she won't share any more about.

What can I do to get better at tuning in and understanding other people's minds?

It can be useful to notice any patterns in the assumptions that you might be making about what other people might be thinking or feeling (see the box earlier in this chapter). Then you can remind yourself that you can't read other people's minds (if only...that would make Sue and Bridie's jobs much easier!). It's normal and human to get it wrong and misunderstand what someone might be thinking, feeling or wishing just because we are busy, but it happens a lot when we are feeling strong emotions ourselves or trying to block them out. If you have the space for thinking about your thoughts and feelings, then you're more likely to be able to catch yourself when your feelings are stopping you from being open to someone else's mind/experience. Other people can be in the exact same relationship and understand it and feel totally different from the other person. Neither is right or wrong, it simply is. This can be hard to accept if you are a logical, concrete kind of person, but it's also what makes navigating a relationship so complex and wonderful.

We have to use our imagination fully to be able to mentalize. Other people's minds are hard to make sense of. They often don't understand their own stuff, as we know it can sometimes be hard to work out why we might behave/feel respond in particular ways. Also, the things about minds is that they can change or be influenced, so when trying to mentalize, it is totally normal to get things wrong. The important bit is about being curious and trying to make guesses rather than deciding you have cracked it. You need to gently check out your understanding, and then adapt (or update) your understanding when new information becomes available. Be flexible. Similarly, other people might not know what you are thinking, so help them out! Tell people how you are feeling, thinking, and what you need. Make it OK for when you check out how they might be feeling or thinking too. The box below has some questions that you can ask yourself when you're trying to better understand the mind of another person and make sense of their behaviour in a situation. This is not a quick quiz. Try to work through the questions one at a time, to deepen your understanding and make guesses about the reasons behind their behaviour. The main ones Bridie likes to use when she is checking-in with herself or there are intense emotions or if she is struggling to tune in are, 'What am I feeling and why am I feeling this way *right now*?' and 'What is really going on for them?' They are simple, but they help to ground you and keep you curious.

STOP AND PAUSE

Take a minute to calm your emotions before reflecting. Questions to ask yourself:

How do you make sense of what just happened?

How were you feeling during the situation? What were you thinking? Why might you have been feeling the way that you were?

Do you think that you might have made an assumption of how the other person was feeling, based on your own feelings and beliefs?

Try to put yourself in the other person's shoes and imagine the situation from their perspective. Did the other person react differently from you? If yes, what do you think might be the reasons why they reacted differently?

What do you think the person might have been thinking and feeling about the situation? Write down as many guesses as possible.

If you could have seen thought bubbles coming out of the top of their head, what do you think might have been in them?

What do you think they might have been wishing for?

What do you think the other person might have wanted from you?

What do you think they might have thought you were feeling or wishing for at the time? How might they have felt about that?

What do you think the person might be thinking or feeling about the situation now?

Notice, has the other person been trying to make the situation better in any way, to make things OK with you or show you that they care?

Also, notice if the other person is struggling themselves. They might be caught up in their emotional mind, finding it hard to make sense of the situation or might have their own difficulties that they're struggling with.

Having made guesses about what the other person might have thought, felt or wished, are you able to see the situation in a slightly different way? What might be a more balanced way to view the situation?

It can be useful to ask yourself mentalizing questions when you are struggling with a relationship or interaction, and either having or receiving an intense emotional response. It's especially useful if there is ongoing conflict and you want to try to mend or repair a relationship. It can be useful to go through the questions with someone who is close to you, or whom you trust. They might be able to help you change your position or increase your curiosity, or they may simply offer another interpretation of the person's thoughts, feelings and wishes that helps you to understand their responses. When you have made some guesses, it can be worth checking these out with the other person and letting them know how you're feeling (see Chapter 12 for tips on how to have these conversations), so that you can try to get a shared understanding of what happened. This can really make you feel closer to important people, make them (and you) feel understood, and make it easier to move forward and find a solution if you need to. Often just the understanding of the misunderstanding and the connection that this brings is resolution enough.

Bridie has a recent example of where she has had to use her mentalizing skills.

Bridie was feeling quite angry and upset with a friend. This friend had let her down numerous times, when they had planned to meet up and the friend had cancelled at the last minute. However, the friend had continued to keep in touch, express her regret and arrange to meet up again. Then, Bridie was having an important celebration, and the friend said that they were coming, but then cancelled at the last minute, making up an excuse. Bridie felt frustrated and really let down, as if the friend saw her and their friendship as unimportant.

Initially, Bridie felt that the friend was just being a poor friend. But, when she took the time to reflect, she realized that she was just seeing the situation from her own perspective, and she was probably partly thinking from her emotional mind. She then started to imagine other possible interpretations, and what her friend might have thought or felt.

My friend probably felt quite bad that she had to cancel, and quite guilty. Maybe this is why she left it until the last minute to tell me, because she was avoiding having to tell me.

I suppose that she might have struggled to get to the celebration.

She might have been struggling to afford it, but didn't want to say.

She does struggle with anxiety in social situations, and she wouldn't have known anyone there, so perhaps she was feeling fearful about going. Maybe she was going to try to come along as she didn't want to let me down, but it felt too overwhelming nearer the time.

Maybe she didn't realize how important it was to me for to her to be there.

Maybe we have different views of our friendship and how close we are.

Bridie then tried to think about how her friend had been trying to make things better and noted that she had perhaps ignored these initially.

She has apologized a lot. Although it has been over messages (but this might be because she doesn't want to face me/is scared is feeling bad). She has tried to make other arrangements to see me and has said that she will try to fit around me. She has offered to meet to do things that I want to do.

Bridie initially didn't feel particularly kindly towards this friend, but once she had done the earlier reflections, she was able to think in a kinder, more balanced way. Bridie was then able to express to her friend how she had felt about the situation in a gentle way and check out her understandings of her friend's perspective with her.

How to practise mentalizing

You can also practise your mentalizing skills by watching foreign movie clips and tuning in to all the non-verbal things that help you work out what the character is intending, thinking and feeling (then turn on the subtitles!). There are no right or wrong answers, as it's an imaginative exercise, so it should be fun. If you insist on being serious and making it relevant to your life, then you can also think through recent situations, reflect on and make guesses about what other people might have been thinking or feeling, and where possible, check out your understanding with them in a tentative way. For example, *'I noticed that when I spoke to you earlier, you seemed frustrated with me. I wonder whether this is because I was asking you to go out with my friends again and you don't want to go. Maybe you feel that we always go out with my friends and do what I want to do, but you prefer to stay in at the weekends when you can, as you're tired from work. Am I getting any of this right?'* The other person might agree with what has been said and that they do feel frustrated that they have been asked to go out again. Or they might say that they were just tired so had not been feeling frustrated but just a bit overwhelmed with work. Or that they're actually looking forward to going out with you and your friends, as it's a bit of a break and that they did not mean to seem frustrated. All of these responses help you to 'get' each other. It's absolutely fine for you to get it wrong as long as you make it clear that you are just making guesses. No one ever likes being told what they think or feel by others – trust us, we are psychologists who have thoughtlessly made this mistake a couple of times! Also, trust us that, usually, the other person just feels important and pleased that you're trying to understand them a bit better.

Some clarifying questions that you could ask could be:

- I noticed that... Is that right?

- Is everything OK with us? It feels as if...(I've upset you/You're angry with me/and so on).

- How are things between us?

As a quick summary of a complicated area, try to remember that the minds (thoughts, feelings, intentions and wishes) of other people are just as complicated as yours but a bit more difficult to see. They can feel confusing to you, but also possibly even to themselves, because they could well be struggling with recognizing their thoughts or feelings in the moment just like you do, and might be caught up in their own emotions. Minds can also change in an instant! So, the best you can do is understand that you can't 'read the minds' of others, but you can stay open, interested and curious and then make guesses about what they might be needing, thinking and feeling. Be aware that you could be making assumptions or falling into traps based on your own feelings and thinking errors. Then take time to think it through and see if you can use your imagination and all the clues you have to see them from the inside and yourself from the outside.

⋛ Chapter 12 ⋚

Saying No and Being Assertive

The need to have relationships and closeness with others is an important part of being human. As humans, we crave connection with others. It's part of our biological make-up. But, as we know, relationships are fragile. They need nurturing and effort to keep them strong, and we need to repair any damage along the way. This chapter will therefore consider the following key relationships skills:

- Building positive relationships.

- Assertiveness: being able to assert your view/say no/ask for something.

- Repairing a relationship.

- Recognizing when relationships aren't healthy anymore.

We often learn these key relationships skills from those around us growing up, such as our parents or carers. But when these key adults have struggled with these skills themselves it can lead to us struggling too. Unfortunately, these difficulties can be passed down in generations. For example, if Katy's Mum had lots of unhealthy relationships, Katy might have started to see that these are normal and therefore might be more likely to put up with unhealthy behaviours in her own relationships. If Pete's Dad never said sorry when they had an argument, and just pretended that nothing had happened, then Pete is unlikely to know how to repair relationships himself. If Scheana's foster carer never said what he felt and avoided conflict at all cost, how would Scheana know how to be assertive and express her views in a helpful way? So, sometimes we need to take time to learn these skills ourselves and try them out in our own relationships.

Building a positive relationship

When we think about how to build a positive relationship with someone, it can be useful to think about what we, ourselves, would want from other people. How would we want them to be with us? What would make a good friend? Or a good partner? What would make us want to spend time with someone, feel close to them and want to stay around?

Some of the main attributes that we often want from those around us are: understanding (someone who understands or 'gets' us), accepting (not judging us, making us feel good and not bad), a good listener (someone who wants to listen and seems interested in what we have to say) and someone who makes us want to smile. In DBT, we call these GIVE skills.

(be) **G**entle
(act) **I**nterested
Validate
(use an) **E**asy manner

Gentle

Start being gentle, by making sure that your tone of voice is calm and engaging. Be respectful to other people and avoid judgement (as much as possible!).

Interested

Try to take an interest in the other person. Ask questions. Be curious, about them, their views, interests, wishes and desires. Really listen. It's rare that as humans we take the time to really listen. Often as we are listening, we can end up interrupting or talking over the other person. This can just make them feel ignored, that we don't really care, or we aren't listening. Instead of this, try really listening to someone (pause, ask them questions about what they have said). See how this feels. It can be really tricky to do (as you might want to jump in and interrupt) but can also help the other person to feel connected to you and understood by you. It can help if your body language also shows that you are interested. Put your phone away! Then, face the person and give them good eye contact, keeping open body language (make sure that you don't seem closed off).

Validate

Validation is how you show the other person that you 'get them', and that their feelings, wishes and needs are understood by you. You can do this by saying out loud how you understand them in a non-judgemental way. For example, 'That must be really hard' or 'That must have been upsetting for you'. This can help the other person to feel understood and that it's OK for them to think and feel what they do, and that you don't judge them. When you validate, you aren't trying to cheer the other person up or sympathize with them (e.g. saying, 'At least he didn't dump you' or 'At least you didn't fail it all'). Instead, you are trying to acknowledge and sit with the emotion that the other person is feeling (i.e. empathizing). This is one of the most powerful ways of connecting with another person – 'they get me'.

For example, Sue once experienced the death of someone close to her. She was really upset about it and missed them a lot. Many of her friends tried to cheer her up, saying things like, 'At least they had a good life' and 'At least they're not in pain anymore.' Although they were trying to be helpful, this made Sue feel that they didn't understand what she was going through, and that it didn't feel OK for her to grieve (she felt that it was almost as if they expected her to be grateful for what had happened). Then one of her close friends messaged her to say, 'That's really shit, I'm so sorry.' Sue felt that this friend understood where she was at, she knew that she could be open and honest with them and trust them with her true feelings, and she felt comforted.

Easy manner

When we talk about an easy manner, we mean trying to be someone who is generally nice to be around. This can be someone who smiles, might use humour and has relaxed body language; someone who is easy to approach. If this is something that you struggle with, maybe spend some time practising doing this around people. In DBT they talk about 'leaving your attitude at the door'. So, if you're feeling in a mood, maybe take a few deep breaths and try to relax your body and your face, allow your mouth to form a gentle smile and step forward. Have a go, have a practice, and see how it works. It can also be useful to observe people who you think do this well, and see how they do it, so that you can try to act in the manner that they do. When you first act something and then practise doing it, you will start being able to do it more easily and naturally over time (although it can feel a bit weird at first). When you act in an easy manner, you might see that people also change their reactions towards you and they might become more positive, which makes it easier to keep this up.

Assertiveness

We talk about three styles of communication: passive, aggressive and assertive:

Passive	Assertive	Aggressive
Putting up with things despite not liking them or feeling comfortable with them.	Raising concerns with others and trying to address them in a helpful way.	When people act in a way that doesn't feel right, letting them know but sometimes becoming angry doing this.
Ignoring own feelings and pushing them aside.	Giving views, but also listening to the views of others.	Refusing to back down...ever.
Trying to just go along with whatever the other person wants. Putting other people's views and wants first.	Expressing feelings and needs at an appropriate time and with the most appropriate person.	Trying to control what happens in relationships – only one way of doing things.
Avoiding conflicts at all costs or giving in quickly if challenged.	Negotiating and finding a compromise.	If people don't listen, getting frustrated and angry, possibly shouting or storming out.
Looking down/avoiding eye contact, smiling, even if feeling rubbish, making self small.	Making good eye contact. Using confident body language.	Being quite intimidating to others – staring, shouting, standing up, aggressive body language.

We might use all of the above communication styles at one time or another, and they can all be useful in different situations. But the style that is generally seen as the most helpful for effective communication with others is an assertive style. This is where you're able to put forward your own needs and emotions, while still being aware and mindful of the needs of others. The following few skills therefore are based on assertiveness – being able to express your needs in a helpful way.

Managing your emotions in the moment

Before going into an interaction with someone, where you want to express a view, it can be useful to help yourself to feel calmer first. Check-in with yourself (How am I feeling right now? Do I need to do anything to feel calmer?). If you're feeling any strong emotions such as anger, frustration, annoyance, sadness or anxiety, perhaps take a few moments to help yourself to calm down. This might mean walking to make yourself a hot drink, taking a few breaths, or even first talking it through with someone else whom you can trust, to help you to think through what you want to say.

It might be that the person you want to talk to has really upset you, or hurt you, and you want to let them know how much; or that they have done something to really wind you up and you just want to punch them. When you are feeling really emotional about something, it can be hard to articulate yourself clearly and think about the other person's responses. If you think that they don't 'get it', it can lead you to feel even more emotional (and even more likely to start crying or punch them in the face!).

When you're ready, you can use the following tips to express yourself clearly and ensure that your view is heard in a helpful way.

Saying no

There are two main steps to help you to say 'no' to someone about something. The first step is to express your understanding of the other person's wants (*validate*), but then state clearly that you do not wish to do it (*assert*). That's all. Although it might be tempting to explain why you don't want to do something, it's much clearer and simpler (and less easy to argue against) if you just say that you would prefer not to do it. Good phrases to say include, 'I don't feel comfortable with...' or 'I'd prefer...'

Some examples include:

'I know that it's a beautiful day to go to the zoo, but I'd prefer to stay at home today.'

'I can understand why you want me to save my money up for a car, but I'd prefer to spend it on clothes this month.'

'It's lots of fun when we go out with your friends, but I don't feel comfortable staying out all night again.'

At first, it may feel really difficult to say no to things, especially if you're used to just agreeing, so it can be useful to practise. Start saying 'no' to people about small things that you feel comfortable with and that feel quite easy to do, then slowly work your way up to bigger things that might feel more uncomfortable to say 'no' to.

Getting what you want out of an interaction

In DBT, there's a skill you can learn that can help you to get what you want out of an interaction with someone and assert your view. This skill is named DEAR MAN, and consists of:

Describe the situation in a factual manner.

Express how you feel about the situation (e.g. I feel...).

Assert your position and state clearly what you want.

Reinforce what will happen if the person does what you're asking them to (i.e. what will be in it for them).

(be) **M**indful about what you're asking for and try to stick to talking about this without going off on a tangent. Be a bit of a 'broken record' if you need to be.

Appear confident throughout, keeping good eye contact, open body language (shoulders back) and speaking clearly.

Negotiate and try to find a solution that is suitable. But also remember that you can agree to disagree and end a conversation if needed.

DEAR MAN can be a useful skill to have and to use across a range of scenarios where you need to be assertive, ask for something or say no to something. It can be helpful when planning out what you're going to say or writing a message to someone. When Sue used to support a group in Wales, she worked with the young people to think about how they could use DEAR MAN skills to ask for a Nando's takeaway for the last group session. This could look something like this:

> Hi Amanda
>
> Our last group session is coming up, and we were wondering if we could have a Nando's takeaway for the lunch please (*describe*). We all love Nando's, so feel that it would be such a lovely treat and a good way to celebrate the ending of the group (*express*). Perhaps we could look at the budget to see if this is possible (*assert*)? It would be great if you could join us too and be part of the celebrations (*reinforce*).
>
> Should we check-in with you next week to see if there's any money available for this (*mindful*)?
>
> Best wishes
>
> The DBT Skills Group

If you're planning to use this skill in person, it can be worthwhile first thinking through what you want to say, and how you might say it, as it can be difficult to think on the spot when you are first learning how to use it. However, as with all relationship skills, it will become easier over time and with practice.

Repairing a relationship

As we said, relationships are vulnerable things. They're sensitive to events, experiences, perceptions and transitions. They can change, flex and adapt, but they're also often fragile and can break down. Even when we are using all our positive skills and strategies, we can be taken off guard, make an absolute mess of an important interaction and hurt (or be hurt by) the people we love. So, one of the best and most important relationship skills that we can have is to be able to repair relationships – the ones that we want to maintain. Once mended, they can become stronger, more adaptable and resilient.

Have a think. If someone was to hurt or upset you, how could they make things better with you? How could they show you that they care?

Have you had a relationship breakdown in the past that has been repaired? Or a time that you have fallen out with a friend, family member or partner and then been able to make up afterwards? If yes, what helped the repair?

If it's a recent argument or blow up, it might just take a small show of affection or care to repair it, for example making the other person a hot drink or apologizing for your part in what happened.

Sometimes it can be an apology (if this feels genuine). If there's still some disagreement, there can be an acknowledgement of this, and an expression of a wish to move forward. For example, 'I know that things have been really difficult between us recently. You don't agree with the way that I treated your friend Anna, but I don't think that I could have done anything differently. So, we feel a bit stuck. Our friendship is really important to me, so I am hoping that we can try to find a way for us to move forward.'

It can be the case that you will not ever agree with what a person did and feel hurt by it, but if you want to repair things, then it's important that they know that you still think they're OK and that the relationship is important. When people feel that interactions are blaming and personal ('you are bad' rather than 'I really didn't like it when you did that'), then it's hard to make the repair.

There might also be times when a relationship has become unhealthy, or even toxic, and you might want to move towards ending the relationship rather than repairing it.

SAYING NO AND BEING ASSERTIVE

Recognizing when relationships are not healthy

When we talk about unhealthy relationships, we think about ones where at least one person is not being treated with respect, and one person usually has more power in the relationship than the other.

WARNING SIGNS OF AN UNHEALTHY RELATIONSHIP

☆ The person has tried to stop (or has stopped) you leaving the house, going to work or seeing your friends or family.

☆ They make unreasonable demands for your attention – want you to be with them all the time, and get jealous/ angry if you're spending time with someone else.

☆ Your access to money, food, drinks and day-to-day items has been restricted – they may tell you what to, and what not to, eat or drink.

☆ They constantly check up on you, check your phone or control what you're doing all the time, such as wanting to know where you are every minute of every day, or telling you where you can or can't go.

☆ If in a romantic relationship, they unjustly accuse you of flirting or cheating on them.

☆ You're pressured to do things that you don't feel comfortable with.

MY INTENSE EMOTIONS HANDBOOK

☆ They put you down, criticize, belittle or humiliate you.

☆ They threaten to hurt you, themselves (or other people), leave you or damage your property if you don't do something that they want you to do.

☆ They blame you for their behaviour, deny what has happened or make you doubt your judgement (sometimes called 'gaslighting'). Or they admit that it happened, but blame their past, their drug or alcohol use or their mental health (such as 'anger problems') for their behaviour.

☆ You might feel as if you're walking on eggshells because you're afraid of what they might say or do.

If you recognize *any* of the above warning signs, this might be an indication that you are in a toxic relationship, and it's important to talk to and seek support from people you trust. If you feel unsafe in the relationship, or want help to get out, there's information in Chapter 13 on organizations that can help.

LUCY'S STORY

A few years ago, I was in a toxic relationship. I remember one day being at the canteen in work and he suddenly told me to, 'Stop talking when you're eating, you're making me feel sick' in front of my colleagues. It was just so embarrassing. It was something that you don't expect your boyfriend to say. It was something more like what your parent would say to you when you were little. It made me feel upset, annoyed and so, so small. He spoke like this a lot. He used to talk about food, and the way that I ate, and would tell me that I was eating too much, that I shouldn't eat particular things as they had too many calories, and that I shouldn't eat when I wasn't hungry. Or if I ate a piece of cake, he'd say I shouldn't have what I'd brought in for lunch. It made me feel like crap and believe that I was fat and horrible. But actually, looking back, I was the skinniest I'd ever been. I lost so much weight when I was with him and became too skinny. But I still felt fat. When I went out with my friend, I would end up crying every time in the toilets. It all felt too much, I felt shit about my weight and how I looked, and I didn't like myself anymore. I started to scratch with my nails on my legs and stomach, where I felt fat, but where people couldn't see it. At times, I realized that things weren't right and thought about leaving him, but I was worried that I was never going to meet anyone else.

Eventually I left him, and now when I look back, I can see how horrible the relationship was and I'm really glad that I left.

Part 4

PUTTING IT ALL TOGETHER

Now it's time to put all your learning together into a self-care plan. It might be that you've picked up some tips from the chapters in this book. You might also have your own strategies that you use that will help you to make your plan. So, Part 3 has a chapter about how to get extra support (and what might be available), including talking to professionals. The last chapter is then about pulling together your self-care plan.

≳ Chapter 13 ≲

Getting Extra Help

Although this book gives lots of ideas and tips about how to manage overwhelming emotions and difficult relationships, we would *always* recommend that you let someone know how you're feeling so that they can support you with it too. This could be a friend, a family member, a trusted adult or a professional (such as your GP). They can then also help you to get more help that you might need, such as therapy.

It can also be helpful to think about who you want to talk to, what you might want to say to them, and how they can help you. For example, knowing that you can call them when you're having a stressful day might be helpful. Or you might not know what support you might want or need, and that's OK too.

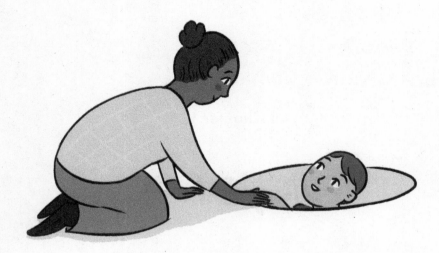

Sadly, sometimes people aren't as helpful as you'd like them to be. Occasionally, people try to 'solve the problem' rather than listening to your worries and validating your feelings. This can be a difficult (and infuriating) experience but it's a manageable one! It's important to remember that somebody having an unhelpful reaction to you talking to them doesn't mean that your feelings and struggles aren't valid. Lots of people struggle to talk about or connect with difficult thoughts and feelings, so they struggle to be helpful to those in distress. Sometimes, you might have caught somebody 'off guard', and in the moment they were unsure of how to react. This doesn't mean they don't care and can often mean that they're worried about worsening the situation and want to think carefully about their response. If it feels difficult for your loved one to understand, a good way to move forward is to be clear about the things that they can do to help. It might be just being there to listen, coming with you to the GP or getting into a new activity with you, or just being on the end of the phone when you need a welcome distraction.

While some people might struggle with talking about and supporting you with your difficult feelings, you can be sure that there will be others who will be happy to offer you support and compassion. Remember, this is mostly about them and their ability to talk about and manage their own feelings rather than a reflection on you or a judgement of your character. If your first attempts aren't successful, try someone new or approach a mental health professional.

Talking to professionals

Talking to friends and family can feel daunting but sometimes speaking to your GP or other health professionals presents its own challenges. Often the clinical setting of a doctor's surgery or therapist's office can feel scary and overwhelming. It could be helpful to bring someone along with you, such as a trusted friend or family member, to support you throughout the appointment (and remember the stuff that goes out of your head when you feel stressed and anxious). While this can give you the confidence to go and see someone, you might need to let the person know beforehand how much input you want them to have in the actual appointment. For instance, you might want to explain your feelings yourself and not be 'spoken for'. Typically, a doctor will ask you some questions about how you're feeling and how long you have been feeling that way. Sometimes they will give you a few questionnaires to fill in so that they can get a better idea of what your individual problems are and how they can help you.

Your doctor may suggest you see a counsellor, attend therapy or consider taking medication to help with some of your problems. If you're unsure of any of the things they're discussing, it's always OK to ask. Appendix II also has a brief guide to medication for young people experiencing intense emotions.

Useful websites

https://stayingsafe.net/intro – Managing self-harm and suicidal thoughts.

https://youngminds.org.uk – Support and information about young people's mental health and medication.

www.ptsduk.org/what-is-ptsd/children-and-young-people Information for young people about post-traumatic stress disorder.

www.talktofrank.com – Information about substance use.

Useful apps

Smiling Mind – A guided meditation and mindfulness app with lots of different exercises and programmes, developed by psychologists and educators with the aim of 'bringing balance to your life'.

Calm Harm – uses DBT skills to help users to resist or manage the urge to self-harm. It helps users to 'learn to ride the wave' using activities: comfort, distraction, expressing yourself, release, random and breathe. Developed by a consultant clinical psychologist for young people.

Helplines and contacts

YoungMinds Crisis Messenger Service (UK only) – supports young people up to the age of 25 years when they're experiencing a crisis and need support. Open 24/7 and tries to get back to someone within five minutes with a trained volunteer. If you need to access this service, send a text message to 85258. www.youngminds.org.uk.

Samaritans: 116 123 or jo@samaritans.org or by the Next Generation Text Service (for people who are hard of hearing) – information available at www.samaritans.org.

Toxic relationships

If you are feeling scared in your relationship, you feel that you need some confidential advice or want to talk to a professional, these are useful contacts:

- Your GP (who will put you into contact with services in your area that can help).

- Women can call 0808 2000 247, the free 24-hour National Domestic Violence Helpline run in partnership between Women's Aid and Refuge.

- Men can call the Men's Advice Line free on 0808 801 0327 (Monday to Friday 9am to 5pm) or ManKind on 01823 334 244. In the UK, men can also email info@mensadviceline.org.uk, which can refer men to local places that can help, such as health services and voluntary organizations.

- In an emergency, please phone the police, or go to the emergency department at your nearest hospital.

≳ Chapter 14 ≲

My Self-Care Plan

These templates can be downloaded at www.jkp.com/catalogue/
book/9781787753822

What I can do to feel OK in my body:

(see Chapter 6)

Patterns that I might get stuck in in relationships:

(see Chapters 4 and 5)

Possible exits from those patterns:

(see Chapters 4, 5, 11 and 12)

How I can soothe my emotions:

(see Chapter 7)

Strategies I can use to ride my emotions:

(distraction/mindfulness /etc. – see Chapter 8)

How I can cope in a crisis:

(TIPP/STOP – see Chapter 9)

Who are the best people to help me:

What other people can do to help:

What I can tell myself:

Note: Remember, if things go wrong this time, it is OK to pick yourself up and try again.

⋛ Appendix I ⋚

Template for a Formulation (see Chapter 2)

My story

What's happened to me? (What are my life experiences that might have triggered intense emotions?)

(For example, losing someone, being bullied, arguments at home.)

What am I really scared of? (What pain/fear might I be trying to avoid or protect myself from?)

(For example, being rejected or let down by others, or my emotions being too overwhelming/out of control.)

What am I doing to cope in the best way I know how? (What am I doing to cope with the fears above? How am I protecting myself against them?)

(For example, keeping others close to me/seeking reassurance that they care or keeping others at a distance and coping by myself, using self-harm or eating a lot to make myself feel better.)

What are the unintended consequences of my ways of coping?

(For example, people get frustrated with me and pull away, which leaves me feeling even more rejected and let down or my emotions build up and then I get suddenly angry/aggressive, or I feel guilty and want to hide my self-harming and hate myself even more.)

What are my protective factors? (What helps me to cope in a positive way/feel better?)

(For example, my close friend Becky, I enjoy my job most of the time, although I don't get on with my parents, I love spending time with my grandparents, I like walking in the countryside.)

A Brief Guide to Medication

Dr Turlough Mills, Consultant Psychiatrist

The use of medication for young people who meet the criteria for emerging personality disorder, BPD or EUPD

In writing this brief overview, I have drawn extensively on the NICE guidelines for the management of BPD (www.nice.org.uk/guidance/cg78/evidence/bpd-full-guideline-242147197). NICE stands for the National Institute for Health and Care Excellence, which is a UK organization that provides guidelines for healthcare and other professionals working in the National Health Service (NHS). These guidelines are recommendations for how healthcare professionals should best care for specific conditions and are reached by a process that involves analysing all available scientific evidence for particular treatments. Guidelines are kept under review and updated in line with new research findings. NHS services should follow NICE guidelines in their practice.

The full BPD guideline runs to 557 pages and discusses contributing risk factors for developing BPD, best methods of assessment, and its psychological and pharmacological (medications) management. There is also a dedicated chapter on the management of BPD in the under-18 population (who I will refer to from now on as 'young people'). I would encourage those readers who are interested in this subject to read this chapter (and indeed the rest of the guidelines). Understanding what child and adolescent mental health services (CAMHS) should be offering you can be a helpful starting point for accessing the care that you need.

The use of psychotropic medication in BPD

NICE guidelines have found no evidence for the effectiveness of any medication in the treatment of BPD, apart from very time-limited use of sedating antihistamines (usually promethazine) for the short-term alleviation of anxiety.

There is, however, recognition that young people with BPD can suffer from co-morbid mental illnesses, such as depression, anxiety and psychotic illness. In these cases, the co-morbid illness should be treated with reference to existing NICE guidance.

Despite this clear guidance, young people with BPD who do not meet the threshold for diagnosing a co-morbid mental illness, will often find themselves in discussion with psychiatrists (and other health professionals) about the use and effectiveness pf psychotropic medication. They may also find themselves taking one or more medications, particularly if they have had an inpatient admission. These medications will often be prescribed off-label, which means prescribing outside the scope of the medication's licence. For example, the second-generation antipsychotic quetiapine is licensed for the treatment of mania and psychosis. Using quetiapine in the treatment of anxiety would be an example of off-label prescribing.

Most of the evidence (as reviewed by NICE) for medication efficacy comes from trials of drugs in adult subjects. This means that lots of psychotropic medications are only licensed for use in adults and their use in under-18s would automatically be off-label.

Young people with BPD, who are suffering and who are in psychic pain, may very understandably want access to medication with the potential to alleviate this suffering. Professionals, who are likely to feel anxious about the risks posed by their patients (usually to themselves), may consider medication as a 'last resort', particularly as a way to try to avoid an escalation of risk, an admission to hospital or other outcomes perceived as adverse. In these instances, professionals are less likely to be treating BPD as a whole, and may rather seek to try to manage aspects of their patient's presentation, such as impulsivity, aggression or mood swings.

One problem with this approach is the lack of good, robust, scientific evidence for it. Young people may end up on multiple medications (with associated risks of adverse side-effects) and if there are then improvements seen, it can be very hard to understand what has led to those improvements. It may be due to one medication in particular, or the combination, or some other non-pharmacological factor or factors.

Sometimes psychiatric medication can make symptoms worse. For example, some antidepressants have been associated with increased suicidal feelings and actions in young people.

This is not to say that medication should never be considered. Different people tend to respond differently to medications. One person may find something helpful, while another may not. Using medication in the treatment of symptoms associated with BPD will always be an exercise in trial and error.

With that in mind, the next sections will briefly discuss medications commonly encountered in the treatment of BPD symptoms.

Sedating antihistamines

This class of medication is the only one that has a sufficient evidence base to be recommended in NICE guidance.

The most commonly used sedating antihistamine is promethazine. It is used for the short-term treatment of acute anxiety and also insomnia. Your doctor may suggest that you try this if you are struggling with acute periods of distress, particularly if they are leading you into acts to self-harm or carry out other destructive behaviours. Promethazine has quite a strong sedating effect, which comes on quickly (within an hour) and you are likely to feel sleepy after taking it. This medication can be very effective at bringing someone down from a highly distressed state, especially when other coping strategies have not been effective.

It is advised for short-term use only (periods of up to a week). When people take medications that have an immediate effect, particularly to make an unpleasant state of mind better, there is always some risk of them becoming dependent (either physically or psychologically) on medication to make themselves feel better. Medication can seem like an easier and more effective method of reducing anxiety and distress than other psychological and behavioural strategies. However, over time, medication will become less effective as your body becomes used to it, leading to a state of tolerance. Medication for the acute alleviation of distress also does not help your difficulties in the long term, and used over a long period of time can make these problems worse.

Antidepressant medication

There are several classes of antidepressants, each of which works in a different way on the brain. The most commonly used by far are selective serotonin re-uptake inhibitors (SSRIs). Fluoxetine is in this class, as are sertraline, citalopram and mirtazapine. Only fluoxetine is licensed for the treatment of depression in under-18s, although other medications are used.

SSRIs block the breakdown (re-uptake) in the brain of the neurotransmitter serotonin. When they were first discovered, it was thought that there might be a very direct link between being in a good mood and serotonin levels. SSRIs were described as 'restoring chemical balance to the brain'. However, with subsequent scientific study, the link does not seem as clear as it was initially. Although SSRIs start working on the brain immediately, the effects on mood often take quite a bit longer to appear (weeks rather than days). Some people seem to find SSRIs very helpful, others less so.

People who are severely depressed, who struggle to concentrate or get out of bed in the morning, who have lost interest in things they previously had enjoyed and consistently see no point in living, appear to be those who benefit most from antidepressants. Sometimes people describe that they seem to disrupt cycles of negative thinking and give them more energy to do things, and they seem most effective when they help people access psychological therapy.

NICE guidance recommends the use of antidepressants in the treatment of clinical depression when it exists with BPD. Antidepressants are not thought to be helpful in the treatment of BPD alone. In fact, as they are associated with an increased risk of suicidal thoughts and actions in under-18s, they can sometimes make things worse.

It is not uncommon for young people to receive an initial diagnosis of depression or anxiety, only for that to be changed later (maybe even in adulthood) to BPD. This can be very distressing for the young person and their families and may indicate years of ineffective treatment. It reiterates the importance of formulation in diagnosis.

Antipsychotics

Antipsychotic medications are used primarily in the treatment of psychosis and mania.

Psychotic states are characterized by delusions, hallucinations and a lack of insight, which are all indicators of a person's profound departure from consensual reality. Mania refers to persistent and significant elevation of mood, associated with insomnia, reckless behaviour and lack of insight. There may be overlap between mania and psychosis. Both manic and psychotic presentations indicate that someone is severely unwell and are associated with mental illnesses like bipolar disorder and schizophrenia.

Lacking insight means being unaware of how ill you really are, or even believing that you are not ill at all. Someone who is not able to realize that they are unwell, while at the same time not being in touch with reality, might get themselves into some very dangerous and risky situations. NICE guidance recommends immediate treatment with antipsychotic medication for someone who is acutely unwell with psychosis or mania.

First-generation antipsychotic drugs work primarily by blocking dopamine receptors in the brain. They can cause a range of side-effects, including parkinsonian symptoms (tremor and involuntary movements), which may be irreversible and can have life-threatening complications.

Second-generation antipsychotics (which include olanzapine, quetiapine and aripiprazole) act on a range of receptors in the brain and each medication tends to be associated with its own set of side-effects, including weight gain, changes in heart rhythm, changes in metabolism (and associated risk of diabetes) and a risk of death.

Antipsychotics have a strong tranquilizing effect, which can cause a relatively rapid reduction of symptoms. Once symptoms are brought under control, a person may need long-term treatment with antipsychotics (sometimes for the rest of their lives).

Because of this tranquilizing effect, they are sometimes used off-licence to treat agitation and disturbance associated with other conditions, including delirium, anxiety, eating disorders and BPD.

In BPD, antipsychotics might be used to try to treat symptoms of impulsivity, aggression or mood swings. They may also bring some relief by alleviating or dampening persistent negative thinking. However, there is very little evidence, if any, for using antipsychotics in this way. Treatment is usually determined by your psychiatrist's previous clinical or anecdotal experience, and there may be significant variation between services (including inpatient units) and from psychiatrist to psychiatrist. Second-generation antipsychotics tend to be used more frequently as they are considered to be safer.

They should only be used under careful medical supervision with appropriate physical health monitoring. Unlike treatment for schizophrenia or bipolar disorder, antipsychotic treatment should be short term.

Mood stabilizers

Mood stabilizers are used in the treatment of bipolar disorder. This is a serious, usually life-long mental illness, characterized by periods of mania and periods of severe depression. These periods are often extreme, usually last for weeks or more, and often require intensive treatment, which may need to take place in hospital.

Antipsychotics, anticonvulsants and lithium are all considered to be mood stabilizers.

This chapter has already discussed antipsychotics. They are often used to treat acute manic episodes, especially those with psychotic features. However, they can also be used as longer-term mood stabilizers in-between episodes (with the intention of reducing frequency and intensity of episodes).

Anticonvulsants are used in the treatment of epilepsy and are also used as mood stabilizers. They are associated with some significant health risks and require careful monitoring by a doctor.

Lithium treatment is also associated with health risks and requires regular blood tests, including checking that levels in the blood are neither too low nor too high.

Mood stabilizers may be used off-licence in the treatment of BPD. Some people may find them helpful for severe mood swings and impulsivity. As second-generation antipsychotics such as quetiapine and aripiprazole are considered safer than both anticonvulsants and lithium, these are likely to be more used more often in the under-18 population.

Benzodiazepines (sedatives)

Benzodiazepines include drugs like diazepam (valium) and lorazepam. They were at one time used to treat anxiety. They work on GABA (gamma-aminobutyric acid) receptors in the brain which are the same receptors that alcohol also works on. They are very effective at relieving anxiety. Unfortunately, they are also addictive and cause physical and psychological dependence quite quickly. For this reason, they are not recommended in the treatment of BPD.

They may very rarely be used in the inpatient setting for the immediate relief of extreme agitation. However, as they can sometimes paradoxically make agitation worse, medications like promethazine or second-generation antipsychotics tend to be used instead.

Summary

Although the evidence only supports the short-term use of promethazine as a way to manage agitation in BPD, sometimes other medications may be used as well. Different people may find different medications helpful at particular times in their lives.

It is important to have a full discussion with your psychiatrist about the risks and benefits of such medications, and to make plans for treatment to be as short term as possible.

REFERENCES AND

FURTHER READING

Allen, J. (2018). *Mentalizing in the Development and Treatment of Attachment Trauma: Developments in Psychoanalysis.* London: Routledge.

American Psychiatric Association (2013). *Diagnostic and Statistical Manual of Mental Disorders* (fifth edition). Washington, DC: APA.

Barnes. C. M. & Drake, C. L. (2015). 'Prioritizing sleep health: Public health policy recommendations.' *Perspectives on Psychological Science,* 10, 6, 733–737.

Bateman, A. & Fonagy, P. (eds) (2019). *Handbook of Mentalizing in Mental Health Practice* (second edition). Washington, DC: American Psychiatric Association.

Baumeister, R. F. & Leary, M. R. (1995). 'The need to belong: Desire for interpersonal attachments as a fundamental human motivation.' *Psychological Bulletin,* 117, 497–529.

Beckes, L. & Coan, J. A. (2013). 'Toward an Integrative Neuroscience of Relationships.' In J. A. Simpson & L. Campbell (eds), *The Oxford Handbook of Close Relationships* (pp. 684–710). New York, NY: Oxford University Press.

Blakemore, S. (2018). *Inventing Ourselves: The Secret Life of the Teenage Brain.* London: Transworld Publishers.

Bowlby, J. (1969/1982). *Attachment and Loss, Vol. I: Attachment.* New York, NY: Basic Books.

Bowlby, J. (1980). *Attachment and Loss: Vol 3. Loss: Sadness and Depression.* New York, NY: Basic Books.

Brukner, L. (2014). *The Kids' Guide to Staying Awesome and in Control: Simple Stuff to Help Children Regulate their Emotions and Senses.* London: Jessica Kingsley Publishers.

Brukner, L. (2016). *Stay Cool and In Control with the Keep-Calm Guru: Wise Ways for Children to Regulate their Emotions and Senses.* London: Jessica Kingsley Publishers.

Coan, J. A., Beckes, L. & Allen, J. P. (2013). 'Childhood maternal support and neighborhood quality moderate the social regulation of neural threat responding in adulthood.' *International Journal of Psychophysiology, 88,* 224–231.

Coan, J. A., Schaefer, H. S. & Davidson, R. J. (2006). 'Lending a hand: Social regulation of the neural response to threat.' *Psychological Medicine, 17,* 12, 1032–1039.

Collins, N. L. & Feeney, B. C. (2000). 'A safe haven: An attachment theory perspective on support seeking and caregiving in intimate relationships.' *Journal of Personality and Social Psychology, 78,* 1053–1073.

Domes, G., Heinrichs, M., Michel, A., Berger, C. & Herpertz, S. C. (2007). 'Oxytocin improves "mind-reading" in humans.' *Biological Psychiatry, 61,* 731–733. doi:10.1016/j.biopsych.2006.07.015.

Eisenberger, N. I., Master, S. L., Inagaki, T. I., Taylor, S. E. et al. (2011). 'Attachment figures activate a safety signal-related neural region and reduce pain experience.' *Proceedings of the National Academy of Sciences, 1081,* 11721–11726.

Feeney, B. C. & Kirkpatrick, L. A. (1996). 'Effects of adult attachment and presence of romantic partners on physiological responses to stress.' *Journal of Personality and Social Psychology, 70,* 255–270.

Fox, N. A., Henderson, H. A., Marshall, P. J., Nichols, K. E. & Ghera, M. M. (2005). 'Behavioral inhibition: Linking biology and behavior within a developmental framework.' *Annual Review of Psychology, 56,* 1, 235–262.

Gardner, M. & Steinberg, L. (2005). 'Peer influence on risk taking, risk preference, and risky decision making in adolescence and adulthood: An experimental study.' *Developmental Psychology, 41*(4), 625–635. doi:10.1037/0012-1649.41.4.625.

Gerhardt, S. (2004) *Why Love Matters.* Hove: Brunner Routledge.

Harlow, H. (1958). 'The nature of love.' *American Psychologist*, 13, 673–685.

Hofer, M. A. (2006). 'Psychobiological roots of early attachment.' *Current Directions in Psychological Science*, 15, 84–88.

Hirshkowitz, M., Whiton, K., Albert, S. M., Alessi, C. *et al.* (2015). 'National Sleep Foundation's sleep time duration recommendations: Methodology and results summary.' *Sleep Health*, 1, 1, 40–43.

Irons, C. & Beaumont, E. (2017). *The Compassionate Mind Workbook: A Step-by-Step Guide to Developing Your Compassionate Self.* London: Robinson.

Linehan, M. M. (2015). *DBT Skills Training Manual* (second edition). New York, NY: Guilford Press.

Logue, S., Chein, J., Gould, T., Holliday, E. & Steinberg, L. (2014). 'Adolescent mice, unlike adults, consume more alcohol in the presence of peers than alone.' *Developmental Science*, 17(1), 79–85. doi:10.1111/desc.12101.

Lopez, F. G., Melendez, M. C., Sauer, E. M., Berger, E. & Wyssman, J. (1998). 'Internal working models, self-reported problems, and help-seeking attitudes among college students.' *Journal of Counseling Psychology*, 45, 79–83.

McCormick, E. W. (2008). *Change for the Better: Self-Help through Practical Psychotherapy* (third edition). London: Sage.

McKay, M., Wood, J. C. & Brantley, J. (2007). *The Dialectical Behavior Therapy Skills Workbook: Practical DBT Exercises for Learning Mindfulness, Interpersonal Effectiveness, Emotional Regulation and Distress Tolerance.* Canada: New Harbinger Publications.

Mikulincer, M., Gillath, O., Halevy, V., Avihou, N., Avidan, S. & Eshkoli, N. (2001). 'Attachment theory and reactions to others' needs: Evidence that activation of the sense of attachment security promotes empathic responses.' *Journal of Personality and Social Psychology*, 81, 1205–1224.

Rathus, J. H. & Miller, A. L. (2015). *DBT Skills Manual for Adolescents.* New York, NY: Guilford Press.

Reddy, V., Hay, D., Murray, L. & Trevarthen, C. (1997). 'Communication in Infancy: Mutual Regulation of Affect and Attention.' In G. Bremner, A. Slater & G. Butterworth (eds), *Infant Development: Recent Advances* (pp.247–273). Hove: Psychology Press.

Sbarra, D. A. & Hazan, C. (2008). 'Co-regulation, dysregulation, self-regulation: An integrative analysis and empirical agenda for understanding adult attachment, separation, loss, and recovery.' *Personality and Social Psychology Review*, 12, 141–167.

Siegel, D. J. (2010). *Mindsight: The New Science of Personal Transformation*. New York, NY: Bantam Books.

Siegel, D. J. (2018). *Brainstorm: The Power and Purpose of the Teenage Brain*. London: Scribe Publications.

Simpson, J. A., Rholes, W. S. & Nelligan, J. S. (1992). 'Support seeking and support giving within couples in an anxiety-provoking situation: The role of attachment styles.' *Journal of Personality and Social Psychology*, 62, 434–446.

Snyder, D, K., Simpson, J, A. & Hughes, J. N. (2006). *Emotion Regulation in Families: Pathways to Dysfunction and Health*. Washington, DC: American Psychological Association.

Treisman, K. (2017). *Working with Relational and Developmental Trauma in Children and Adolescents*. London: Routledge.

World Health Organization (2018). *International Classification of Diseases for Mortality and Morbidity Statistics* (11th revision). Geneva: WHO. Retrieved from https://icd.who.int/icd11refguide/en/index.html?r

INDEX